CW01593960

Sustainably Stylish

FIRST EDITION

SHERYL BOLDEN

Copyright © Sheryl Bolden, 2021

Sheryl Bolden asserts the moral right to be identified as the author of this work in accordance with the Copyrights, Designs and Patents Act 1988.

A catalogue record for this book is available from the British Library

Text © Sheryl Bolden 2021
Design © Jump Web Services 2021
Illustrations © Elvina Choi 2021
Cover Design © Irene Burley 2021
Infographics © Rhea Reburiano-Lajom, 2021

All rights reserved. No part of this publication may be reproduced, stored in a retrievable system, or transmitted, in any way or by any means, electronic, mechanical, photocopying, recording or otherwise without prior permission of the author.

This book is sold subject to the condition that it shall not, by way of trade or otherwise, be lent, re-sold, hired out or otherwise recirculated without the authors prior consent in any form of binding or cover other than that of which it is published and without a similar condition including this condition being imposed on the subsequent purchaser.

ISBN: 978-1-914288-41-8

Printed and bound in China on FSC paper

For more detail on the book and the author visit
www.makemywardrobework.com
Instagram @makemywardrobework
Facebook Make My Wardrobe Work

DEDICATED TO DAVID

For always believing in me and accepting that there will always be room in the wardrobe for one more handbag.

Contents

Introduction 8

Notes to the reader 10

Part 1

Context

1 Cost Per Wear 15

2 The Art of Investing (or Acquiring) Well 27

3 Sustainability Unwrapped 47

4 The Changing Face of Retail 63

5 Faster, Cheaper, Easier 73

6 Fashion & Ethics 83

Part 2

Your Wardrobe & Your Style

7 Creating your Style and Loving your Look 95

8 How to Edit your Wardrobe 107

9 How to Shop your Wardrobe 125

10 Looking Good for Less 135

11 Caring for your Clothes 143

Part 3

Shopping

12 Sales, Glorious Sales 155

13 Love, Preloved 167

14 Fabric Matters 187

15 End of Life 209

16 What's the Alternative? 223

Final Thoughts 238

About the Author 244

Acknowledgments 246

References 248

Introduction

'Sustainable Fashion' is most definitely in vogue. Marketing campaigns urging us to reconsider how we consume our clothes are everywhere. From social media posts to magazine adverts, from podcasts to documentaries, the message is clear,

"Shop Sustainably"

But what is sustainability when it comes to shopping and, more specifically, fashion?

Despite being frequently used and marketed, it is a complex and nebulous term. For many, 'sustainable' fashion is an oxymoron.

This book looks at what 'sustainability' within the fashion industry is and discusses the concept of fast and cheap fashion and why it's become so prevalent, whilst introducing some realistic solutions and alternatives. As well as empowering you to become a more conscious consumer, I've also filled this book with 'how to' chapters on everything from redefining your style, editing your wardrobe, looking good for less, to successfully shopping the sales and buying preloved.

The fashion industry faces ethical and environmental challenges, from a lack of regulation to inequitable sourcing practices. Its' impact cannot be underestimated, and there is no doubt it must undergo systemic change to become more sustainable. But the idea that we, as individuals, can solve problems created by a multi-billion-dollar fashion industry alone is ridiculous. I've focussed on the things that we can control and suggest steps that we can all take, to make a real difference.

This isn't an anti-fashion or anti-shopping book. I love shopping and I love clothes. I love them like some people love cooking, gardening, or a particular sport.

For me, clothes are a passion. They are an expression of who I am, what I love and what I stand for. But I want to add to my wardrobe in a way that limits harm to others and the environment. I want to inspire you to do that too.

I've included fashion related quotes and other ditties by myself and others, to inspire and amuse you along the way. This book is also part anecdotal and explores my relationship with, and love of clothes, and I'm excited to share this with you.

Notes to the Reader

This book doesn't need to be read from front to back. I've grouped the chapters into three interlinked sections, sequenced in a way that makes the most sense to me, but you can read in any order that suits you.

There is a general list of references at the back of the book, quotes have for the most part be attributed within the text but where the source of information is particularly useful I have placed it as a footnote on the same page, personally, I find that more helpful.

- Throughout the book I talk about 'clothes' but what I am referring to **also encompasses shoes, bags, accessories and everything else** you might wear.

- When I mention monetary value, I have **referenced British pounds** throughout. While USD maybe the global currency of trade, I felt that in the context of retail, the use of dollars could create confusion in value, for readers in Hong Kong.

- When I talk about sustainability practices and challenges within the industry, **all views, unless indicated, are my own.**

- This book **does not hold all the answers,** I hope that I make it clear just how nuanced and complex the subject is. There is **no one solution to tackling the huge problem of over consumption and resultant waste** we face globally.

PART 1

Context

Buy less,
Choose Well,
Make it Last

VIVIANNE WESTWOOD

1

Cost *Per Wear*

I deliberated for so long over which chapter to open with, and despite the temptation to dive straight into what sustainability is and means, within the context of our clothes, I decided against that and choose to open with 'Cost Per Wear', as the concept is fundamental to the way I shop. For me the notion of wearing our clothes for longer, is one of the foundations of creating a sustainable wardrobe.

I believe it is important to think of your clothes as an investment. Fear not, I'm not talking haute couture, luxury watches and top tier designer hand bags - you'd naturally expect the value, and hence your investment of those high-ticket items to appreciate over the long term. I'm referring to the clothes that you buy, you should demand a return on your investment, regardless of their price tag.

You have invested your time, hard earned money, and some level of emotional energy into buying something that you are going to wear. Aside from loving it, like everything else you purchase, it should deliver value.

Measuring this value, in a financial sense, is known as Cost Per Wear, a term I assumed was in everyone's vocabulary! I naively thought that this was a concept everybody not only understood, but used. However, in talking to friends and clients, I've learned this isn't the case. Let me explain.

Cost Per Wear (let's refer to it as CPW), is a simple calculation to determine your sartorial Return on Investment (ROI). Basically speaking, this is the total cost of the item purchased, divided by the number of times it is worn. The lower the CPW the better your ROI!

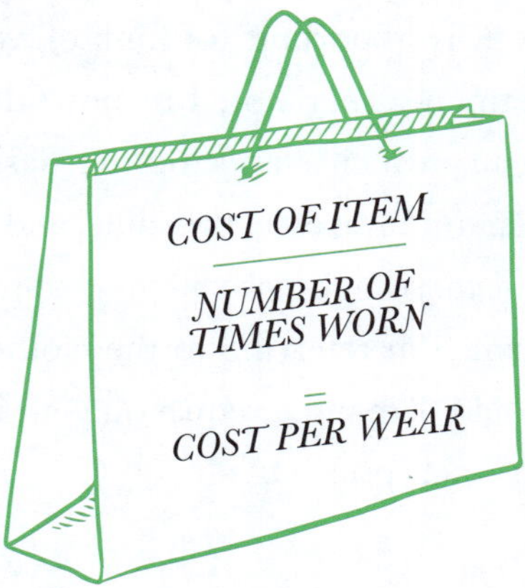

Without doubt, a low CPW is good for the bank balance. Wearing our clothes more frequently is an important step in becoming more sartorially sustainable, but it isn't the only one. There are a variety of factors that contribute to how sustainable an item of clothing is. To assess these, I've coined the term, '**Sustainability Return**' this isn't a scientific or academic term, rather my own informal way of considering a wider range of factors that help to assess how sustainable my choices are. I thought it would be useful to you too.

While the CPW is focused solely on the number of wears, my **'Sustainability Return'** also considers

- The material an item is made from.
- How long an item will be used for.
- How and where it was made.
- How I can dispose of it or move it on when I no longer want it.

The number of resources, environmental, human, and economic that are required to make even the simplest of garments should not be underestimated. Let's look at what it takes to make a pair of jeans – a true wardrobe staple!

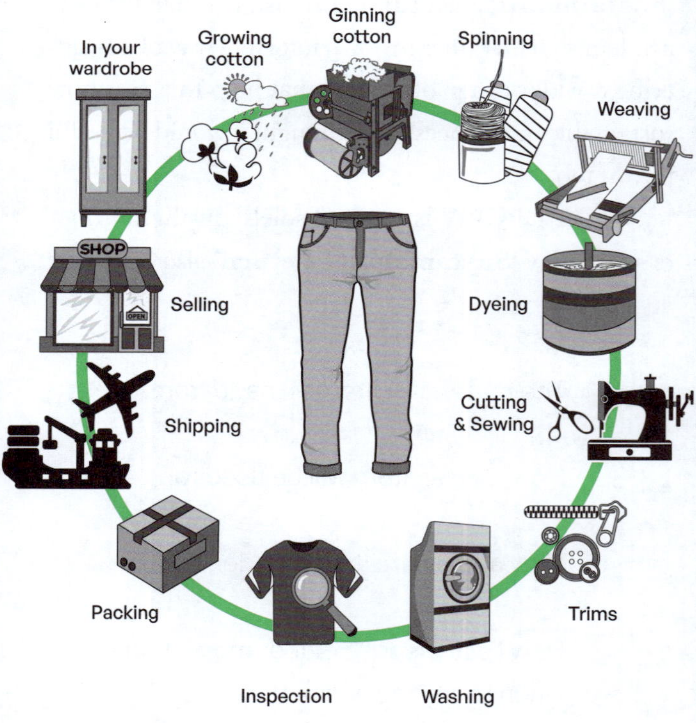

Jeans are usually made of cotton, which is grown, harvested, ginned, spun, and dyed before being weaved into denim, which is then sent to a factory to be cut and sewn. Buttons, rivets, and a zip are added, followed by washing, and sometimes bleaching before the finished garment is ready to be inspected, packed, and transported, then unpacked and distributed, and then finally sold to you. The proud new owner!

Hundreds of people are involved in creating that one item. It really takes your breath away.

By only wearing these jeans a handful of times, before throwing them 'away', all the resources used, both natural and human, as well as the emissions created throughout the entire supply chain, will have been in vain. What a waste! (The reason I say 'away' is that there is no such place, but we'll get to that later).

A better Sustainability Return is achieved when we keep a piece of clothing in circulation for longer, this is because the investment of resources used in producing the item is amortised with each wear.

But let's get back to Cost Per Wear – My justification for buying new clothes!

More often than not, we end up with a high CPW because we invest in the 'wrong' clothes. By that I don't mean we buy awful, ugly clothes - I'm not here to judge your sartorial choices. What I'm referring to, is spending a lot of money on the types of clothes that rarely get worn.

Occasion wear is a great example of an area of our wardrobe that delivers a low ROI. Occasional dresses and the like tend to be expensive and are worn infrequently – so let's talk through a familiar scenario.

You are attending the wedding of someone special and naturally, you want to look fabulous, so decide to buy a new outfit. You shop around, do your research and find 'the dress'. For the sake of this example let's say the price tag is £200 - not an insignificant amount of money, but you love it and you can make the numbers work, so you buy it.

You rock it at the wedding, manage not to ruin it with red wine, nor rip it during some crazy dance move. Success!

A few months later, you change up the heels and hair, giving it a sexier look for a birthday party, which is attended by a different set of friends. Another change of accessories, and the addition of a jacket, and the dress is perfect for a christening. So far so good. The dress of your dreams has had three outings!

Before you know it, Christmas has arrived and your company is hosting a posh party, so out it comes again.

You still love the dress, but you are starting to think it would be nice to wear something different, but then you feel guilty that you spent so much on it and no one at work has seen it yet. Your conscious gets the better of you and just like that, you have chalked up four wears.

In the new year another occasion to wear said dress arises, but by now you are bored of it. Your friends have seen it, and your social media is full of photos of you wearing it. The print is distinctive so you decide, despite a hefty cost per wear of £50, to retire the dress and buy something new in the January sale, (more on that pitfall later.)

We'll get to the solutions that can improve the CPW wear of that kind of purchase, in a moment, but first, let's look at the other end of the spectrum. There are some things that we buy that deliver a really low CPW.

Let's exemplify an average a pair of work trousers. Imagine you work, study or volunteer in an environment that requires you dressed in relatively smart way. Despite knowing that trousers are a strong, versatile, year-round staple, you instinctively resent spending money on 'work' clothes, so you shop about on the High Street and pick up a classic pair for £45.

The fit is okay, and they do the job, but you don't feel amazing when you wear them. Nevertheless, during their first year, you wear them on average twice a week, for 35 weeks. As they enter their second year, the poor quality and frequent washing starts to show, they get saggy at the knees and bum. The fabric starts to bobble, and unfortunately, the button pops off!

As a result, you only wear them once a week for the first three or four months of that year, before finally admitting that they don't look good and get rid of them.

In total you wore them 86 times, with a CPW of 52 pence! Without a doubt, that's a pretty good ROI. There is no denying you got your monies worth from those trousers, but two things come to mind.

Firstly, loving the clothes you own and feeling fabulous when you wear them is incredibly important to me. With these trousers, you just couldn't get excited about them and never really loved wearing them. Was it really money well spent?

Secondly, despite the low CPW, there is a high chance these trousers didn't score well against my Sustainability Return. Due to the price, I'll assume the fabric was a petroleum-based synthetic, probably weaved in one country, transported to a second (low labour cost) country to be produced, and then shipped to a third country to be sold on your High Street. That's a pretty high carbon footprint for something that was only worn for 18 months!

That's before we even consider what happens to the trousers when you throw them 'away'. The poor quality of the garment means you can't pass them on to a friend. It's unlikely a charity shop would want them. Sadly, this means that their final destination will be (and it needn't be) landfill. Items like this may cost you very little per wear, but they carry an unreasonably high impact.

To improve your Sustainability Return, I'd suggest spending more wisely on the trousers. By investing in better fabric and all-round quality, you'll receive a more flattering fit, the trousers should last longer and hopefully you'll love them more! This means wearing them more often, and not merely seeing them just as 'work trousers', offsetting any increased cost.

Shopping with a brand that's ethically sound is likely to reduce the negative environmental and social impact of producing those trousers, so even if the cost per wear remains equal, the Sustainability Return will improve, and you will love the clothes you own - #winwin.

It goes without saying that CPW makes economic sense. But for me, its importance from a sustainability perspective cannot be underestimated. By using CPW, we are encouraged to think about clothing's long-term use and return, rather than the immediate gratification of buying something that you don't truly love, just for the sake of having a new top to wear on a Saturday night. We've all done it...

Love the clothes you wear

SHERYL BOLDEN

The chances of loving your look ***increases when you buy clothes you truly love***

SHERYL BOLDEN

2

The Art of *Investing (or Acquiring)* Well

It's all very well understanding and using cost per wear to value your clothes so to speak. But how can you ensure that you only buy clothes that you love enough to want to keep wearing for years to come?

To help you to do this I'm sharing my ultimate pre purchase check list. These are the questions, which I always mentally ask myself before making any purchase. Not adhering to this check list is often the reason why we don't love, or wear something in our wardrobe.

I'll go through each one in more detail but please, if you take nothing else away from this book, commit this handy check list to memory and never hand over your cash or card until you are certain you have satisfied all the criteria. I promise, it really will make a difference.

1. Does it **fit you**, right now?
2. Do you **love it on**?
3. Will you **wear it three ways**?
4. Are you **happy with the quality**?
5. Can you **afford it** – and the **potential maintenance**?

Does it fit you, right now?

Too many people underestimate the importance of fit so let's tackle that first. When you try something on, ask yourself honestly, does this fit me? And I don't just mean, can I physically get into it, does it sit properly in the right place? Are your boobs where they should be, is the length right? Does the waist on the garment sit where yours does? And what about the shoulder seams?

If it fits you well, exactly as it is, then bingo, it's an absolute winner. Ignore the next paragraph and move on to question two!

If the answer was no, don't dismay, there a few scenarios to consider:

It's only a smidgen too small and the rest of the check list is positive.

In this case it's only a slightly risky purchase. If you believe that it will soon fit without too much effort or by a simple alteration, and the rest of the check list answers positively, then it's probably a good buy.

It's far too small and you can't get it done up.

Without pointing out the obvious, you literally cannot wear it – and yes with a strategic change of diet and lifestyle you may slim into it, but honestly (and I'm not judging!) it's a big gamble. If you do buy it, it's likely said item will become the 'Debbie Downer' of your wardrobe, looking at you every time you see it shouting, "I knew you'd never fit into me"! This does little for your self-esteem, not to mention the valuable space it will take up in your wardrobe. My advice, if it is any more than half a size too small, put it back. Alarm bells should be ringing re this risky purchase.

It is too big?

When this happens to me, I am both gutted and delighted in equal measures! I very much doubt your first thought will be, "I must put on some weight so this fits me"! If you really love it and there are no smaller sizes available, you may consider having it altered. Tailoring, especially in Hong Kong, is often convenient and inexpensive. I highly recommend it. However, always consider the complexity of the alteration. Some are easier than others and the cost will reflect this. The amount you spend on any alterations should be added to the initial price for the purpose of calculating cost per wear.

Length is usually the easiest to adjust, as long as the hem is not hugely complicated, shortening can be done inexpensively. Straps are also often a quick fix. As someone who is just shy of 5’3”, I often find that the natural shoulder, where the strap should sit, is a few inches above where my actual shoulder is, leaving an excess of strap and a super low neckline! Usually this is a relatively straightforward alteration, the result of which is that the neckline sits where the designer intended, and I am not flashing my cleavage to the world!

TOP TIP/ EXTRA INFO

If you wondered why a particular brand often fits you really well, well the reason is probably that their fit model (the person or people who try on the clothes so the designers can visualise and amend their designs before an item goes into production) has similar proportions and shape to you, so naturally the style will flatter you. A fit model is often a UK size 12, and normally shorter than the models hired for marketing and press campaigns. Each size is graded from this base size, so that the proportions and look are maintained. Every brand will have a different ideal, and so that is one of the reasons why you can be a different size in a different shop or brand.

A note for pregnancy

During my first pregnancy I made a rookie mistake, I like to think I was not the only woman to do this. Instead of buying clothes from the maternity ranges, I just shopped from my usual brands, but bought the next size up. Not my wisest move I must admit! Maternity clothes are designed to accommodate a growing bump and allow for a slight increase in other areas like your boobs and bum – hardly rocket science, I know! As a result, I ended up with some very ill-fitting outfits, that were tight across my bump but too big across the rest of my body. In the early stages of pregnancy, and with some casual jersey styles that have little structure, you can get away your favourite brands. But as the months progressed it was clear that even one size up was too small and I ended up with clothes that never really got worn. There is a reason maternity clothes are designed the way they are – to fit your changing body, proportionally!

It goes without saying that post-partum your body will change. I mean, you have grown a human and I hope you give your body all the credit and love it deserves for performing such an incredible task. The reality is that some clothes will fit differently, the proportions of your body as well as the number on the scale are likely to change. Don't waste money on something you think will work six months into motherhood. It's likely you will have a whole new perspective on what you want to wear. Wait, and shop then.

2 Do you love it on?

I'm sure that, like me, you've flicked through a magazine and circled something that you think is so gorgeous and perfect, you immediately head to the appropriate website. Let's say it's a fabulously flouncy top, it looks so 'you', and is in stock and within budget that you cannot resist ordering it. Immediately.

On arrival, it is every bit as beautiful as it was on the page but, when you try it on, it's not that it doesn't fit, it's just that it doesn't look quite as fabulous on you as you imagined.

Perhaps the print overwhelms you, the colours don't suit your complexion, or the silhouette doesn't flatter your shape. There could be 101 reasons why something, so good on paper, doesn't quite work in real life. It's at that point you need to be honest about whether you will truly love and wear it.

I like to rank my clothes on a scale of 1-5

Identifying the 'fives' is easy, I love them, always. They make me feel and look great, no matter what. These pieces are not always special occasion clothes, but sometimes they are. They can be a great T-shirt, or the perfect fitting jeans, the shoes that never let you down or a skirt that goes with everything. In essence, they are our favourite go-to clothes.

The 'ones' barely need discussing. They are so bad, that you simply don't own them. If you are only ranking something a two out of five, then you really shouldn't be wearing (or buying) it.

The 'fours' are keepers. Generally, they are items I wear with love and pride but perhaps they only look great in some circumstances, such as with the right hairdo or shoe. Often, they have been worn with such frequency that I have put them into hibernation.

Now for the interesting part, those clothes that rank as a 'three'. When doing a wardrobe edit this is where we spend the most time, 'saving' those items. Don't worry, we'll discuss how to do that too!

The reason I bring this ranking up now, at the point of potential purchase, is that when you are buying something new, it needs to be at least a four. If this new item doesn't score highly, then no matter how beautiful the print, the silhouette, or the colour, if it isn't right on you, you just won't wear it. It will hang in the wardrobe like a piece of art that, despite its beauty, never fulfils its purpose – to be worn with love.

Buying clothes that you truly don't love will never achieve a great CPW. Return them while you can still get your money back. As sad as that may be, your bank balance will thank you, however your friend who normally benefits from these mistakes, will not!

3 Will you wear it three ways?

Will I wear it? A question asked by a million women in changing rooms all over the world. “Yes of course, but I just don’t know when or where - yet” is a common reply we use to justify a purchase. We’ve all done it! The frequency in which you wear something usually depends on two main factors:

1. How practical it is.
2. The number of ways it can be worn.

Let’s start with is it practical?

Often peoples’ first thoughts around practicality relate to its care. “Am I really going to dry clean this work top?”, or “Is it realistic that with a new baby these lovely white trousers will stay white?” Answering these questions is straight forward. What is often neglected is the physical practicality.

Let me tell you about this stunning jumpsuit that I bought. I did and still do truly love it. The fit is flattering. It’s monochrome and so can be accessorized differently, and the shoe combination is endless. I bought it in the sale from a brand I love, whose clothes are out of budget at full price. So far so good. What's the problem I hear you ask? Well, it is impossible, and I mean impossible to go to the toilet solo. As you know, a jumpsuit needs to be pulled down to your ankles to go to the toilet, not the best!

The top part is a strapless bustier which is fastened by hook and eye at the rear, and for added complication, there is a cut out on the back, meaning you can't just pull it back up and fiddle with a zip. Despite many attempts at home, it is not possible for me to unhook then rehook the bustier. Every time, I need the help of a friend to literally unfasten and refasten me into this ensemble.

I discovered this at a wedding, when one of my best friends had the pleasure of this task several times throughout the day. By the time it got to the evening party, she announced that she'd had enough and was delegating the task to a mutual friend!

On a night out with your besties, this is not a big a problem, but hardly something I can task a random in the ladies' loo to do, or on a date night with my husband! As a result, one of my favourites jumpsuits rarely gets an outing. This has indeed reduced its CPW. Let that be a lesson in remembering the practicality of use.

Now let's consider how many ways it can be worn.

I love thinking about this and it's where I get to be creative and experiment. There are countless solutions and ideas about how to wear something differently – not all of them immediately obvious. Of course, there are exceptions - swimwear, nightwear, wedding dresses and true occasion wear – these all have genuine limitations which shouldn't exclude them from purchase.

To improve your CPW, and to avoid the item becoming a one hit wonder, I'd recommend visualising a minimum of three ways you will wear it, before you buy. I'll exemplify a dress, as often this is a garment that women generally think are least versatile.

A friend once gave me a dress, it had only been worn a handful of times, I asked her why she no longer wanted it and her reply was. "it's a printed silk chiffon dress, I've worn it to a few weddings, not much else can I do with it now all our friends have seen it". The dress was gorgeous, so the temptation was to take it and say thank you very much but fortunately for her, I am a good friend and so showed her ways that she could continue to wear the dress and improve her CPW. We chatted about how she could mentally downgrade it from 'special' to 'everyday' and wear it more casually, and thus more often. That weekend I encouraged her to give it a go with trainers and a leather belt. Her natural reply was, "I can't wear a silk dress just to lunch!". She did and she looked fabulous, received compliments, and felt amazing!

Next, I suggested she wear it to work by paring it with a formal blazer and black pumps, giving it a professional twist. She walked into a presentation, felt good and nailed it. Obviously in part because she is awesome at her job, but also, I hope in part because knowing you look good, does wonders for confidence.

In winter I have been known to disguise a dress as a skirt by wearing knitwear over the top. This often works well when a chiffon or crepe dress is teamed with tights and boots. It is a great way to inject colour and interest during a time when it can feel natural to avoid bright colours. More unusually and depending on the style of the skirt half of the dress, I've even put another skirt over the top and showcased just the top.

Naturally some items need little imagination. Jeans for example can be worn any which way, and to almost everywhere. When bought well (fit and quality are King), they regularly return a very good cost per wear.

Even when something fits well and you really love it, if deep down you know you will just never wear it, consider if it is really worth investing in.

I'm such a fan of dresses - they are far more versatile than most people give them credit for. For the days that you really don't want to think about outfit-building or mixing and matching, there it is just hanging up ready to go!

4 Are you happy with the quality?

Now for quality. If you have got this far then it must fit, you really love it on and know exactly how and when you'll wear it. But let's not fall at the final hurdle.

To curate a sustainable wardrobe, you need clothes that can be worn over a long period of time and have been made to last.

Let's use the analogy of buying a car. You'd be meticulous in ensuring the car was fit for purpose and delivering value, perhaps even have a knowledgeable friend check the engine over. While in almost all instances, the value of the clothes will be considerably less than a car, don't forget that this sartorial purchase is also an investment.

So why not use the same approach to quality, and inspect the items asking yourself

- Will it wash well?
- Does it feel nice to touch and to wear?
- Does it look and feel expensive?
- How is the stitching, is it dense, flat, and even?
- Are the hems and the buttons secure?

If the hems or button are falling away, or hanging down, before you leave the shop, then chances are it won't fair well after a few washes or wears. The better the quality, the longer it will last, and in my experience, the more care and attention that was given during the manufacturing stage, the more likely the fit is to be superior.

5 Can you afford it – and the potential maintenance?

I'll keep this brief. I'm not here to advise you on your finances. I'll assume you are savvy enough to make any purchase decision, based on your own financial circumstances and needs.

It would, however, be irresponsible of me not to highlight that cost should be a factor in making a purchase decision. As someone who, in my younger years, got into a lot of debt buying clothes I couldn't afford, on credit cards that cost me more on interest than on dresses, I can attest to the dangers of spending beyond your means on clothes.

If your next purchase makes you look and feel fabulous, fits well, is of good quality (that you can afford) and you know where and when you'll wear it, then make the purchase. I promise you; you'll wear it for years to come! As my late Granny used to say, "*I wish your health to wear it*".

Buy what you love, *not what you should love.*

The most sustainable item is ***the one we already own***

3

Sustainability *Unwrapped*

Before curating your sustainable wardrobe let's discuss what sustainability actually means in the context of clothes, and why we should care.

As one of the world's most polluting and damaging industries, Fashion's impact has rightly been at the for front of global criticism. In 2021, The World Economic Forum report[1] stated that fashion, at about 5% of global emissions, is tied with Fast Moving Consumer Goods as the third most polluting industry, after construction (10%) and food (25%).

But I'm sure that comes as no surprise to you. It has been almost impossible to escape the negative press that the fashion industry has received over the last decade or so.

1 WEF Net Zero Challenge The Supply Chain Opportunity 2021 PDF (weforum.org)

The United Nations 2021 (IPCC) climate report[2] left little room for interpretation. Climate change is real.

The fashion industry is not alone in having to face up to the fact that it must change. For those of us engaged with the crisis, it can often feel overwhelming. Over production, scarcity of resources, the ethical treatment of workers, modern day slavery and water pollution are just a few of the complex challenges that face the industry.

Thankfully, in recent years, there has been an increase in the number of organisations advocating change. NGOs such as Fashion Revolution, Green Peace, Redress, Ellen Mac Arthur Foundation, Sustainable Apparel Coalition, and others have stepped up to inform and educate.

By shining a light on the failings of the sector, NGO's and sustainable fashion campaigners have increased pressure on brands to become more 'sustainable' but what does this mean?

Often, in the context of fashion, many of us associate 'sustainability' with 'green' or environmental issues but sustainability is comprised of three pillars,

2 Climate change widespread, rapid, and intensifying – IPCC — IPCC

Environmental, Social and Economic.

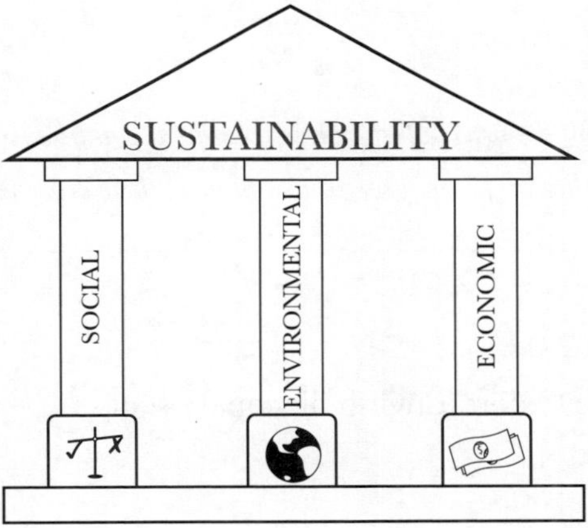

When we talk about how sustainable something is, often what we really mean is how much social, environmental, or financial impact does it have. To be in a position to scale positive social and environment impact, a business must be financially sound and profitable. Positive social impact is about bettering the lives of the workforce and the communities in which it operates. From an environmental position, the impact of producing, or selling should not have a detrimental impact on the local environment.

The 1987 United Nations Brundtland Commission defined sustainability as

> “
>
> *Meeting the needs of the present without compromising the ability of future generations to meet their own needs*

and the Oxford English dictionary states,

> “
>
> *To avoid using up natural resources*

but in the context of fashion, the term is nebulous. Unsurprisingly, there is no one single certification that makes a garment ‘sustainable’. Differing stakeholders embrace a variety of views on what constitutes sustainable, depending on their own interests.

The laws within the fashion industry, encompassing raw materials, labour, and supply chain, are limited and range greatly from country to county. Aside from the well-established accreditations such as Organic or Fair Trade, the fashion industry has few internationally recognised certifications. Unlike the food industry, where regulation in general is tighter, people tend to understand those claims, and perhaps more importantly, for the most part, trust them to be true.

This lack of consensus and rules around what constitutes sustainable fashion has left a lot of room for interpretation, and as consumers we are left confused, frustrated, and vulnerable to misinformation. Another recent addition to our lexicon is 'Greenwashing'

> *When a company or organisation spends more time and money on marketing themselves as environmentally friendly than on minimising their environmental impact*[3]

The phrase was coined in 1986 by environmentalist Jay Westervelt in an essay he wrote which exemplified how a hotel's marketing campaign deliberately deceived its patrons. I doubt he knew then just how widespread

3 What Is Greenwashing? - businessnewsdaily.com

this practice would become and how used his phrase would be. Throughout the 1980's and 1990's it was frequently used to describe a deliberate strategy that oil, automotive, and chemical companies used to mislead consumers. But in the last twenty years it has become synonymous with the fashion industry.

When retailers market and promote their sustainable wares, it can be difficult to know if their claims are wholly true and, if the additional cost that sustainable alternatives demand are justified. Many brands, at all spectrums of the market, have been accused of deliberately using vague or exaggerated language. Misinformation is rife and unfortunately, it comes down to you and me to delve behind the label and ask questions in order to see the full picture.

Friends often ask me if I think the industry is committed to change, especially as its' growth is dependent on us all continuing to consume. My reply is never binary. Not all businesses want to, nor will, change. But in general, I feel optimistic that the tide is turning.

Those brands that want to thrive long term will implement meaningful changes to the way they do business.

At the 2019 G7 summit The Fashion Pact was formed by a global coalition of companies in the fashion and textile industry, including their suppliers and distributors. Members, such as Kering, (owner of multiple luxury brands) Adidas, Chanel, Nike and Inditex (parent company of Zara) committed to a common core of key environmental goals in three areas:

- Stopping global warming.
- Restoring biodiversity.
- Protecting the oceans.

To achieve this they made various pledges, for example, to remove unnecessary and harmful plastics from their packaging by 2030. To seek out more sustainable sources of raw materials. Kering pledged to offset its greenhouse gases by purchasing carbon credits and to commit to full carbon neutrality.

It will take more than money for the fashion giants to become truly sustainable, but it is a step in the right direction, and where luxury goes, the High Street tends to follow.

As we begin to emerge from the Covid-19 pandemic, we are starting to see some brands, big and small, pivoting, and ramping up their sustainability efforts, or at least talking about it!

In 2015 The United Nations adopted 17 Sustainable Development Goals (SDGs) as a universal call to action to end poverty, protect the planet, and ensure that by 2030 all people enjoy peace and prosperity. Sustainable consumption and production are considered critical enough to have been categorised as an SDG in their own right, SDG #12. These 17 SDGs, also known as the Global Goals, are interlinked, recognising that action in one area will affect outcomes in others. From climate action, to increased equalities, to decent work and economic growth to clean water and sanitation, the impact of the fashion industry relates in some way to all 17 goals. The reality is that fashions adoption of the goals as part of a framework for change has been, in the most part, slow.

The more press and explanation the SDGs receive, the better the public's awareness and understanding becomes, which in turn helps to change behaviours and attitudes. The 2019, and recently republished, Ellen MacArthur Paper, entitled 'Completing the Picture – How the circular economy tackles climate change.' states that by adopting a circular economy the fashion industry can help meet SDG #12.

Claiming that the circular economy framework can improve air quality, reduce water contamination, and protect biodiversity.[4]

But what is the circular economy?

Most clothing is produced in a way that is described as a linear economy, this is based on Take, Make, Use and Waste.

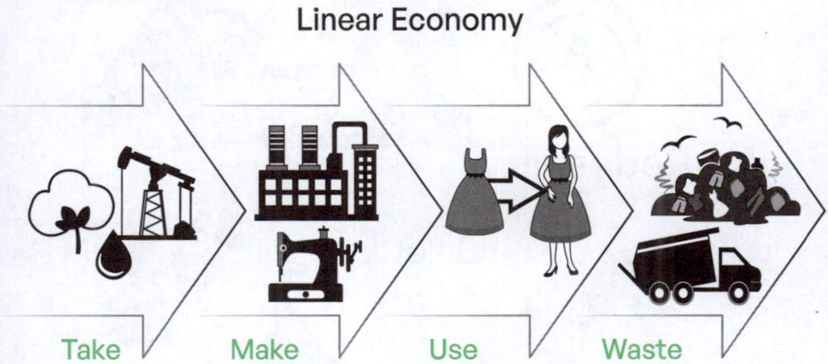

This has been improved a little by the introduction of recycled fabrics and practices, but to be truly sustainable, fashion must move to what is known as a circular economy. Sustainability consultant and founder of Green Strategy, Dr Anna Brismar, defines

4 Completing the Picture - How the circular economy tackles climate change | Shared by Climate Change (thirdlight.com)

circular fashion as *"Clothes, shoes or accessories that are designed, sourced, produced, and provided with the intention to be used and circulate responsibly and effectively in society for as long as possible in their most valuable form, and hereafter return safely to the biosphere when no longer of human use"*. Perhaps the concept is better explained by this infographic,

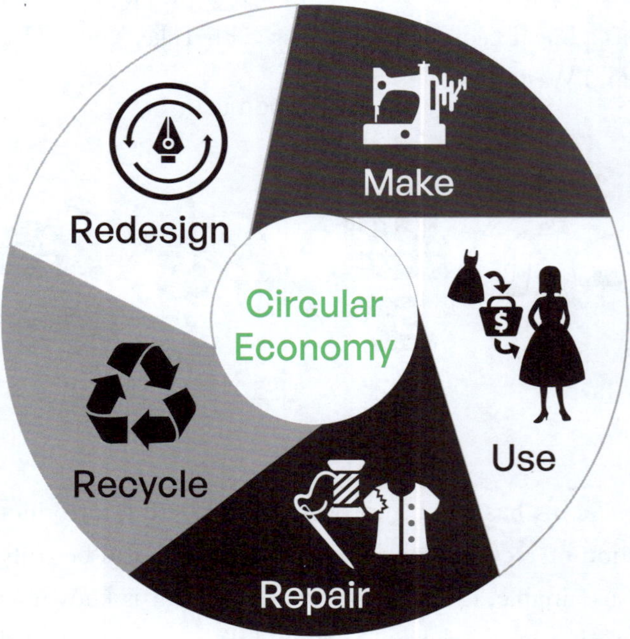

The advantages of moving to a circular model are multiple, reducing pressure on finite resources, stimulating innovation, and removing waste, but

according to a study by McKinsey and the Ellen Mac Arthur Foundation[5], it can also improve productivity and reduce costs, bringing both economic and environmental benefits.

The pressure that both mainstream and social media put on global fashion powerhouses, to change how they do business cannot be underestimated. The role that journalists and activist organisations play in investigating and exposing wrongdoing on our behalf is critical. Especially in relation to increasing public awareness of severe malpractice.

Regrettably these don't always take place in factories located in far flung locations. The recent exposé of factory workers in Leicester, UK, showed that illegal low pay and conditions were rife in the garment producing area that is home to more than 1000 factories[6]. As recently as August 2020, The Ethical Trading Initiative said based on reports by The Environmental Audit Committee[7] and Labour Behind the Label[8], that "*These abuses have not disappeared... it would appear that they*

5 Mapping the benefits of a circular economy | McKinsey

6 Revealed: 'shocking' lack of regulation at Leicester garment factories | Leicester | The Guardian

7 F ixing fashion: clothing consumption and sustainability - Environmental Audit Committee (parliament.uk)

8 LBL-Boohoo-WEB.pdf (labourbehindthelabel.net)

have been exacerbated by Covid-19" Malpractice can be closer to home than many of us like to think.

Disappointingly, the sales of the brands associated with the scandal continue to grow. I wonder if this is really because consumers don't care, or if there is still a real lack of understanding of the consequences of our purchases. Raising awareness and empowering people to make informed decisions was in part one of the reasons I felt compelled to write this book.

There are many small brands who are cautious when it comes to communicating their sustainability endeavours. Some fear by highlighting the aspects they do well, that it will be an excuse for segments of the media to call them out for failing, or not yet succeeding, in other aspects of sustainability. This can damage a brands' reputation, especially if they don't have the resources to respond adequately, and so many brands prefer to say very little, despite doing good work. For me, this is a missed opportunity to help consumers to make better choices.

There are many areas of sustainability that brands can focus their efforts and resources upon to produce more responsibly. This list is by no means absolute, but it will give you an idea of the challenges ahead. The truth is that most brands are not perfect. Very few will excel in all of these areas, but surely it is better to support those that are trying to improve.

1. **The research and development of materials**, that carry less negative impact but can be scaled to mass market.

2. **Garment recycling technology** needs further investment to become scalable and to enable the separation of mixed fibre clothes.

3. **Education and training** in technology that aids zero-waste design.

4. **Adoption of Oxfam's living wage policy** and investment in factories that promote the ethical treatment of workers.

5. **Removal of effluents from local water** supplies and the banning of harmful chemicals from supply chains.

6. **Transferring to renewable energy** sources for manufacture and retail.

I believe that to be sustainable, clothes must be made without negative impact to the planet, to people, and produced profitably and with sound governance. This is possible but truthfully, it is rare on the High Street because it is incredibly difficult to mass produce low-cost clothes profitably, without creating any negative impact.

There are ways to consume fashion more sustainably, and we'll get to those, after all if we are to curate a wardrobe full of clothes, we need to buy something!

Everyone can do ***simple things to make a difference****, and* ***every little bit does count.***

STELLA MCCARTNEY

Sustainability has been ***trending for billions of years****, or we wouldn't be alive. It's* ***excess that is the trend****, and we need to* ***make it firmly out of fashion***

FASHION REVOLUTION

4
The *Changing Face* of Retail

The quote opposite from Fashion Revolution really resonated with me, and whilst this chapter isn't an ode to the 'good old days', I do believe that there's a lot about the way clothes were made, sold, and consumed thirty or forty years ago, that is better than today. So I wanted to explain how todays excess came to be and how the advent of both fast and cheap fashion has changed the retail and manufacturing landscape forever.

Back in my Granny's day, in fact, we don't even need to go back that far, during the 1970's and 1980's clothes were bought to last. Sartorial decisions were not made lightly. Each purchase was carefully considered, not because of a conscious awareness of 'cost per wear', but often due to financial necessity. When money was sparse and new clothes were a luxury, there was an expectation that those bought, would be worn many times. My mum's generation did not consider this to be a sustainable consumption strategy, it was just common sense. Reflecting on those consumer habits now, it really was an unconscious use of 'cost per wear'.

During the 1970s the UK, like many western countries, was a mass producer of textiles and clothes. It was a prosperous and thriving industry. Manufacturers were spread across the country, employing around a million skilled workers[1] who produced a variety of products from jeans to shirts, trench coats to handbags.

British brands used British labour; this was an approach mirrored in many countries, including the USA. While at times specialist fabrics were imported, the clothing itself was frequently made in the country of consumption.

1 Manufacturing a new UK clothing industry (drapersonline.com)

By the early 1980s things were changing, 'offshoring'

> “
>
> *The practice of moving a company's work to a foreign country where labour costs are cheaper*

became a buzzword, that led retailers to totally redefine how and where they made their products. Despite the longer production and transportation time, brands began to manufacture in China. Retailers were more than willing to accept the longer lead time when they saw the affect on their bottom line. The offshoring of manufacturing changed the expectations of a brand's shareholders when it came to profitability. As soon as the brands began to pay less for production, it became difficult to justify paying more.

Back when High Streets were packed with independent boutiques, each town had something different to offer. My family was spread all over the UK and one of the things I enjoyed when visiting various parts of the country, was the different selection of shops. Knowing that I could find something that no one back home would own. I did say that my obsession started at a young age!

Where I grew up, there was a family-owned clothing chain called Ethel Austin, Affectionally known as Ethel's it was founded in Liverpool in 1934 and had branches across the Northwest. It sold inexpensive clothes for the whole family. It wasn't fashion forward nor fancy, but back in the 1980's and 1990's everyone I knew shopped there. I loved popping in with my Nana, and whenever anyone in the family was wearing something new, we would always ask, "did you get it. in Ethel's?"

My best friend's aunt moved to London, and during her regular trips back to Liverpool, she would always pick up a few pieces for her young daughters from Ethel's. On returning home, her trendy London friends would ask her where she had bought all these lovely clothes for her girls from. This was at a time when it was not yet seen as cool, in fashion circles, to buy inexpensively, she would reply that they were from a local brand who had a few boutiques in Liverpool. We laughed that good old Ethel's was earning accolades in one of the fashion capitals of the world.

For me, this was an important learning. It taught me early on how shallow consumers (myself included!) can be. Over the years working in the industry, I witnessed people wearing clothes they didn't like nor suit but chose them solely because of the label inside the garment. These days, I tell anyone who'll listen that when it comes to shopping, "it is not about the name, it's about the clothes".

It's not about brand,
it's about style

Alongside small-scale family-owned chain stores sat more premium and fashion forward boutiques. These local boutiques would, and to an extent still do, buy their stock from the hundreds of independent brands who showcase at exhibitions in London and Europe. Offshoring was a huge factor in the demise of independent retailers, big and small who simply could not compete on price. It became much harder to convince customers to spend more, the product offer and the service had to and still must, be worth paying extra for.

Unsurprisingly, the decline of the independent coincided with the flooding of our town centres with chain stores. Also known as 'multiples', these shops, with tens if not hundreds, of branches all operating under the same name, sharing the same centralised management, and selling the same products either in the same country or globally.

The clothes sold in chain stores were usually competitively priced and mass produced offshore. The lower manufacturing costs facilitated by high volume (more stores to fill) and cheaper labour, led to a general deflation in retail prices. Chain stores became the height of fashion and following in the footsteps of America, supermarkets started to sell clothes, in a 'pile it high, sell it low' strategy. For many, that was the point of no return for retail.

It wasn't just the independents who struggled to compete. The traditional department stores couldn't afford not to move production offshore and so the UK manufacturing industry began to die. By the early 2000s, only 90,000 clothing manufacturing jobs remained in the UK[2].

The way people shopped for clothes continued to evolve and it wasn't only high streets that were struggling, town centres were too. By the early 1990s the out-of-town shopping mall was growing in popularity. The opening of Lakeside in Essex and Meadowhall in Sheffield exemplified a new trend in retail behaviour. These large malls made shopping a past time. Parking was free and easy, and with food courts and cinemas, as well as all the popular fashion and non-clothing 'multiples' under one roof, going to the mall became a day out. Over the next decade malls were built in most major cities and created an ever more homogeneous shopping experience.

This, alongside the rise of e-commerce has, in some ways, contributed to an erosion in personal style and

2 Manufacturing a new UK clothing industry (drapersonline.com)

individuality. We are now all able to access the same brands, selling the same looks, no matter where we live. While there are of course upsides to this, there is the risk this turns us into clones of each other, and in a need to dress 'on trend', we risk losing our creativity and individualism.

One of the positive impacts of e-commerce is that we are starting to see the re-emergence of the independent scene. Nickyl Raithatha, Co-founder of UK-based brand, Finery London, which launched in 2014, saw an opportunity to build a premium High Street offer. He said, "*What we saw since the financial crisis (in 2008) is that a lot of products on the High Street became deflationary, and prices were always coming down*". His brand focuses on creating directional styles with upscale details at a price point slightly above the High Street, keeping 35% of the production in the UK. He goes on to say, "*We don't think of ourselves as fast fashion. The way we operate, it's more like a designer brand. It's not disposable.*"

Another positive of e-commerce is that it has enabled the launch of more sustainably conscious brands and for smaller brands to reach a wider audience, becoming economically sustainable, which shouldn't be underestimated. What is the point of a brand that produces using low impact methods and pays workers a fair wage, if it cannot be financially viable? Social media can help these brands to flourish and grown.

Who knows what the retail scene will look like in another ten years, but I'm hopeful that if consumers like us continue to support brands who do well by doing good, then retail sector will thrive.

Stop buying crap
and companies will
stop making crap.

SHERYL BOLDEN

5

Faster, Cheaper, *Easier*

There is a subtle difference between mass produced, low-cost clothes and true 'Fast Fashion'. The concept of Fast Fashion, some would argue, has been around for centuries. The ability to duplicate high fashion and trends and make them available to the masses is not new. But when I talk about fast fashion, I am referring to,

> *The reproduction of highly fashionable clothes at high speed and low cost. Clothes that are made and sold cheaply, so that people can buy new clothes often.*

The term 'Fast Fashion' was first used in 1989 when the New York Times coined the phrase in reference to Zara boasting that it took them "*15 days between a new idea and getting it into the stores*".

These days there are several brands that are synonymous with, and even blamed for the rise of fast fashion. But did you know that many had been in existence for decades before the phrase was invented? Zara was founded in 1975, H&M in 1947, Top Shop in 1974, and Primark in 1969.

These High Street names, with whom we associate disposable fashion, were instrumental in changing consumer behaviour as well as manufacturing methods and retail business models. But how?

Firstly, globalization allowed these retailers to expand into new markets, brands that you may have previously only shopped at while on holiday, or during a trip to London, began to expand to major cities outside of their home country. This coincided with a rise in consumer demand for frequent low cost, high fashion clothes. These brands delivered and their profits surged, enabling further expansion with scale and pace. They became a fixture in almost every city globally. The beast was born!

By the 1990's the retail strategy of increasing the frequency and speed of new styles to stores was in full swing. A corporate culture of 'sell more, sell more often' had been facilitated by 'quick response' manufacturing. It is impossible to pinpoint just one reason why consumers took to Fast Fashion so readily, but the following are important factors.

Acceptability

During the late 1990s and early 2000s, it became increasingly more acceptable to flaunt your low-cost fashion finds. There was no longer a stigma attached to cheap clothes. Magazines were filled with articles helping to create 'a look for less' and combining high-end pieces with inexpensive fashion was seen as especially savvy.

Accessibility

The expansion of chain stores who specialise in Fast Fashion was instrumental in supporting this new phenomenon. These shops were now on all of our doorsteps', buying fashion was easy. The brands, aided by the media, trained us to expect designer and celebrity inspired pieces in stores, only weeks after their inception.

Fast Fashion was heralded by some as the 'democratisation of fashion'. Enabled by mass production, it allowed more people to participate in 'fashion' regardless of their social and economic background. At this time, credit was cheap and easy, which further facilitated shoppers newly acquired habit.

It is also argued that when Ecommerce took off in the mid-2000s, it further democratised fashion from an inclusiveness perspective. Etailers have been instrumental in widening options for plus-size shoppers, as well as challenging preconceived ideas about what plus-size fashion 'should' look like. I'd argue this was born out of a commercial opportunity rather than a desire to rectify the status quo. There was a gap in the market that mainstream retailers were not filling, plus-sized fashion had not been fashionable or accessible enough and the UK, like many other western markets, was experiencing a physical change in its consumer. The average female waist has grown seven inches since 1951[1] and back in 2013, 45% of British women were a dress size 16 or more, more recent data shows this is a trend that continues to grow. (No pun intended!)

1 Size 12 is Britain's 'ideal' dress size | YouGov

Desirability

Showing off your low-priced purchases became something to be proud of. When H&M opened in New York, retail analyst, Howard L. Davidowitz, writing in the New York Times, said "*It's chic to pay less,*"

He wasn't the only one, fashion editors all over the world were mixing Fast Fashion with haute couture. In 2004 H&M collaborated with fashion designer Karl Lagerfeld to introduce a limited capsule collection, this was a huge success and the collaboration culture – designer label at High Street price, was born.

The launch of weekly glossy magazine, Grazia in 2005 showcased the latest looks from celebrities and brands. Not only did it tell us what 'everyone' was wearing, it also showed us exactly how we could wear it too. Consumer demand was high, and everyone, myself included, wanted the latest look. The fact we could buy it for less, meant we bought more!

The Internet

The 1990s' were a revolutionary decade for digital technology, the introduction of the internet and the World Wide Web changed how we consumed media and later fashion. Fast Fashion brands were able to quickly and cheaply maximise the exposure that they received, when high profile women wore their garments. Further increasing the demand for their products.

Later, the invention of social media led to the rise of the fashion 'Influencer', someone who is able to reach huge numbers of followers, frequently posting aspirational images of must have pieces. These internet sensations further fuelled the obsession with a 'wear once' culture which in turn led to a new crop of even cheaper, predominantly on-line only, fashion brands. In hindsight, given how little understanding and information there was around the negative impact the rise of this type of fashion was having on the environment and many people, it's easy to understand how the phenomenon caught on. Who wouldn't want to buy the most fashionable items for less?

Cheap Fashion v Fast Fashion

We often interchange the terms Fast Fashion and cheap fashion but for me they are not the same thing. Like Fast Fashion, the manufacturing and business model used to facilitate cheap fashion is dependent on cheap labour and materials as well as producing high volume. This low-cost model employed by supermarkets and value retailers is less focussed on selling high fashion trends, targeted the younger and uber cool consumer, and is instead built around the theory that the cheaper something is, the more people will buy.

When analysing why Primark has been so successful, strategist Jeroen Kraaijenbrink wrote in Forbes that they "*clearly compete on price. But it is not just price. It is price combined with an overwhelming large number of fashion items to choose from in their stores. At the bottom line, they sell the kid-in-the-candy-store feeling, the Oh-My-God-I-can-buy-all-of-this-and-still-have-money-left experience. That is their value proposition and that is why they are successful.*"

While cheap fashion is less focussed on the 'wear once' mentality, the reality is that the poor quality usually results in a short lifespan. The race to reduce prices, the pressure on speed to consumer, and the use of emerging markets to produce the goods means many of these garments are inferior in quality and are unable to stand the test of time. These are not the clothes that you can pass down from sibling to cousin, like my mum did. They are designed to be disposable.

What makes the whole cycle even worse, is that to ensure profits remain, the clothes are often made of cheaper synthetic materials, which are almost impossible to dispose of sustainably.

Taking inspiration from the US, around thirty years ago, many European countries witnessed a new trend, supermarkets selling clothes! I remember when the first huge out of town supermarket opened, only a few miles from our house. We could literally buy everything under one roof, going in for bread and coming out with a top or a dress that cost little more than dinner. It shouldn't be underestimated how ground-breaking this was at the time.

These uber low prices, – which often made Fast Fashion look expensive, were facilitated by offshoring production further afield into Southeast Asia, where labour was even cheaper. The sheer volume of customers they served each week, known as footfall, enabled them to sell volumes seldom seen before. The more they sold, the more they bought and the more bargaining power they had to drive down prices with factories.

In order to deliver the lowest price, corners are cut, from the quality to the safety of workers throughout the supply chain. Margins at this end of the retail ladder are wafer thin, and when you are producing or selling hundreds of thousands of a style, every cent counts.

Demand quality, *not just in the products you buy, but* ***in the life of the person who made it.***

ORSOLA DE CASTRO

6

Fashion's *Human Impact*

The apparel industry's impact on the environment and on vulnerable workers across the global supply chain cannot be understated, but when discussing the ethics of fast or cheap fashion it is important to remember that the challenges and issues aren't black-and-white. Solutions are nuanced, complex and varied, depending on perspectives.

When discussing how our clothes are made, the area that naturally, and quite rightly, concerns us most is the health and fair treatment of workers. The pay and conditions of factory and supply chain workers across the developing world, is as varied as the products they produce. The perception can be that some countries are worse than others for housing 'sweat shops', the truth, in my experience is that in all manufacturing countries there are factories that excel and others that fall far below what is considered acceptable.

Some critics of cheap fashion would like to see brands pull out of low-cost regions and cease production in developing countries. But many within the industry argue that communities rely on this work. Without access to these manufacturing jobs, it would lead to further poverty. Not many deny there are few alternatives for mass employment in many of these high population countries.

In order to improve the situation for workers, campaigners believe that workers must be paid more. They advocate for the brands to increase workers' wages, arguing that consumers could and should pay more for their clothes. Chain retailers are often owned by shareholders who demand increasing returns. Brands doubt that consumers, like you and I, will pay more, and so their strategy is to keep growing sales and thus production, in a bid to maintain shareholder profits. To break the cycle of overconsumption, something must give.

A retail strategy of buy less stock and charge customers more per item, would enable revenue and profits to remain. By increasing the price paid to the factory, it would enable workers in the most destitute situations to be paid a living wage and afforded fair working conditions. The counter argument is that, even if cost prices rise, the money paid by brands will not trickle down to those who need it most, instead it will only benefit those already in a position of relative wealth.

It has been said that a disproportionate amount of money is spent on the marketing and promotion, rather than the making of, product. Paying influencers and celebrities alike thousands if not hundreds of thousands of pounds to promote Fast Fashion, while failing to ensure that workers within their supply chain are paid a living wage is a major failing.

According to the Global Living Wage Coalition, a living wage is "*the remuneration received for a standard work week by a worker in a particular place, sufficient to afford a decent standard of living for the worker and her or his family*[1]" A decent standard of living should allow a worker to meet their basic needs, to include food, housing, and other essential needs such as clothing. Even though the cost of living in certain countries may be lower, the salaries paid in the textile industry still do not allow workers to exist with basic dignity, hygiene, or health.[2]

---

1 Home | Global Living Wage Coalition

2 What Is a Living Wage and How Does It Benefit Garment Workers? - Good On You

A major criticism of the pay structure of workers in the textile, garment, footwear, and leather industries, and in global supply chains, is that they are often paid a piece rate and not by time spent on the job. The ILO confirms that, "*In developing countries, workers relying on piece rate wages often constitute a vulnerable section of workers*" In their 2018 report entitled, Piece rate pay and working conditions in the export garment sector[3], the ILO went on to say, "*incentive systems like piece rate wages have been reported to negatively affect the health of workers, due to workers speeding up their production and/or extending their working hours.*" In addition to this, the quality of the garment can suffer as workers are financially incentivised to complete as much as possible as quickly as possible to increase their pay, hence focus on volume and not always quality. As long as the item is 'good enough' to be 'passed' by the person at the end of the line inspection.

Patrick Belser, Senior Economist with INWORK, a subdivision of the ILO argues that,"*Piece rate can be a win-win for both employers and workers, but it needs to be designed in a fair way that is consistent with decent work objectives. Involving workers and trade unions in the design of pay*

3 DP-28-Piece-rate-pay-and-working-conditions-in-the-export-garment-sector_Final.pdf (betterwork.org)

regimes will go a long way to offset some of the negative impacts of piece rate wage systems. There is also a role for governments to provide a robust legislative framework and to ensure that all workers, including those who are paid piece rates, earn at least the minimum wage."[4]

Cheap clothes are synonymous with Bangladesh and the Rana Plaza disaster shook the world. In 2013, it took less than 90 seconds for the Bangladeshi factory to collapse, killing 1,134 people. Unions called it a "mass industrial homicide"[5]. This was indeed a preventable tragedy. According to Human Rights Watch, workers at Rana Plaza were forced to enter the damaged building despite their complaints the previous day about sounds coming from obvious cracks in the building – which then collapsed on them.[6]

Revulsion over Rana Plaza forced brands and retailers to act. This tragedy gave the industry a much-needed wakeup call and led to the creation of two initiatives. The Accord on Fire and Building Safety, made up of mostly European brands, and The Alliance for Bangladesh Worker Safety, largely

4 Piece rate pay brings mixed results for garment workers, new study shows - Better Work

5 Rana Plaza, five years on: safety of workers hangs in balance in Bangladesh | Global development | The Guardian

6 Remember Rana Plaza | Human Rights Watch (hrw.org)

composed of Northern American brands. Both were designed to improve safety dramatically in 2,300 factories supplying western brands.

The Accord was created to enable a working environment in which no worker needs to fear fires, building collapses, or other accidents that could be prevented with reasonable health and safety. It is an independent, legally binding agreement between brands and trade unions to work towards a safe and healthy garment and textile industry in Bangladesh. Since its inception more than 38,000 inspections have taken place at more than 1,600 factories, covering two million workers — with over 120,000 fire, building, and electrical hazards fixed during that time.

The Alliance for Bangladesh Worker Safety was a legally binding, five-year commitment to improve safety in Bangladeshi factories. The Alliance held each member and their factories accountable to operate workplaces that are safe and effective in ensuring building and fire safety. The Alliance ceased operations as planned at the end of December 2018. Its final annual report highlighted some of its achievement.[7]

7 Alliance Fifth Annual Report 2018.pdf (bangladeshworkersafety.org)

- The remediation of 700 factories.

- Fire safety training for more than 1.6 million workers, security guards and factory managers.

- The Alliance's 24-hour confidential worker helpline reached more than 1.5 million workers.

- Alliance-supported Worker Safety Committees has given workers a seat at the table to discuss important workplace concerns, with factory management.

Both initiatives did bring about positive change in Bangladesh, but the dangers persist. All over the world garment workers continue to lose their lives while making clothes. In November 2020, 12 people were killed in an explosion at a garment factory in Gujarat, India[8]. In March 2021, 20 people were killed and dozens left injured after a fire tore through a cloth-

8 Several dead in India factory blast | India News | Al Jazeera

ing factory in Cairo, Egypt[9], with a further eight killed and 29 injured when a 10-storey building collapsed in the same city later that month.[10] Meanwhile, in Gazipur, Bangladesh, one person died and another 42 workers were left injured following a factory fire.[11]

The coronavirus has been devastating for many of us, but according to social scientist and author Dr Sanchita Banerjee Saxena, "*COVID-19 has led to extreme hardship — workers don't get paid enough to actually save anything. They're living hand-to-mouth... there's a whole set of things that haven't changed [since Rana Plaza]—everyday harassment, gender-based violence, the lack of any social protection, the issue of low wages.*"[12]

The encouraging news, and let's end this chapter on a positive, is that NGO's, charities, and the media are shining a light on malpractice, and through social media, momentum for change is growing. Oxfam is calling on consumers to send a message to brands asking them to commit to paying a living wage. NGO's

---

9 Egypt: At least 20 dead in Cairo clothing factory fire | Middle East News | Al Jazeera

10 Eight killed after 'garment factory explosion' | Materials & Production News | News (ecotextile.com)

11 One killed, 42 injured in fire at chemical warehouse in Gazipur factory | Dhaka Tribune

12 Labor, Global Supply Chains, and the Garment Industry in South Asia: B (routledge.com)

such as Clean Clothes Campaign and Fashion Revolution, through their 'Who Made My Clothes' campaign are calling on people like us to hold brands accountable. They believe that you and I have an important and influential role to play. Every time we ask brands questions about how the clothes we buy are produced, we not only demonstrate that we, as consumers, care but we exert pressure on those brands to act.

I believe that together we can make change happen, do you?

PART 2

Your Wardrobe & Your Style

If you wear ***things you adore*** *you just look* ***better***

MARGHERITA MISSONI

7

Creating *Your Style &* *Loving* Your Look

As Yves Saint Laurent once said,

> “
>
> *Fashion fades, style is eternal*

And I wholeheartedly agree! The joy of seasonal ‘must have’ items is short lived, meaning your investment will be too. The pieces you love season after season, year after year, they are the backbone of your look.

One of the things I adore most about clothes, is their ability to allow us to be individual. I love how each person’s interpretation of a trend is a little bit different, and how through our style, each of us can inject our personality into our look. The beauty of style is that we own our own. No one else can replicate it or carry it in quite the same way we can.

Trying to capture what 'Style' means is more complex than I imaged. After referring to my trusty dictionary, I realised the word '*style*' has many meanings. In total ten definitions were found, and four of them could be used in the sartorial sense.

- A distinctive appearance, typically determined by the principles according to which something is designed
- A particular design of clothing
- Fashionable elegance and sophistication
- A confident, effortless manner or technique

I want to make it clear early on in this chapter that I don't believe that having a style means always wearing the same type of clothes or having only one look. You wouldn't want to eat the same food every day, so why would you want to wear the same clothes?

We mix up our menu to include a variety of cuisines depending on how we feel and what we need. Think of clothes in the same way. Different looks for different moods.

Some offer comfort, others nostalgia. At times they are practical, occasionally very special, but often, we just want our favourites that we know and love and that make us feel good.

MENU

Relaxed

Jersey, Activewear, Denim

Sophisticated

Cashmere, Tailoring, Silk

Fashionable

Prints, Statement pieces, Dresses

Evening

Sparkle, Heels, Little Black Dress

People may have said to you, "*I saw an outfit today and it was very you*", but they can't quite articulate what they meant by '*you*'. They can of course describe the outfit and perhaps even compare it to something you already own, but there is always a certain '*je ne sais quoi*', that makes something inherently '*you*'. You may not even consciously know what that is. But subconsciously, it guides the clothes that you love and wear.

Often you can tell when someone is wearing something that isn't quite them, as they often appear self-conscious and can be seen fiddling, faffing, and pulling their clothes mostly down, just to feel more comfortable. This is normally referred to as the outfit wearing them, meaning that the clothes are having a bigger impact than the person.

The old adage that, you should never judge a book by it's cover is true, but it doesn't mean we don't do it anyway. Like it or not, the truth is that people will form an opinion of you based on your appearance.

It's good then to think about what you want the way you dress to say about you. I'll share a tried and trusted method that I found worked well with many of my clients.

Choose three words that you'd want others to use to describe you, not physical attributes, solely words that describe you, based only on the clothes you wear. Go on, give it a try. I think you'll find that it's a thought-provoking exercise and not as straight forward as you'd think – right?

Common style descriptors might include – creative, elegant, approachable, friendly, professional, fun, intelligent, modern, sexy and many more. My choice of words varies, but 'stylish' and 'pulled together' are almost always up there.

When you are editing your wardrobe or pulling together a new combination, or buying new clothes, these words become important particularly if you are unsure if something is 'you'. When in doubt, refer back to these words and ask yourself if the said piece represents how you want others to see you?

It's important to ensure that the clothes you wear now, reflect the person you are today. Very few of us dress the same way now as we did 15 years ago. Your style evolves, just as you do. Use your words to help your look to reflect you. For example, if your chosen style descriptors are - 'refined', 'modern', and 'elegant' but your outfits resemble that of a middle-aged geography teacher from the 1990's, then maybe it is time to re-work your wardrobe.

Re-working your style is not to be confused with getting rid of all your clothes, just because you have had them for years, some of my favourite things are more than a decade old and I still wear them. It's about updating how you wear them and what you wear them with, as well as adding in some new items to create the look you want. Whatever that look might be, it is important that you are comfortable and carry it with confidence.

Feeling confident and comfortable in an outfit allows you to relax and for your personality to really shine through. You'll walk a little taller and smile a little wider, and a smile is always the best accessory.

There is nothing quite like receiving a compliment on our choice of outfit. It makes us feel good, and can leave an impact for many years, I bet you can remember a particular piece that someone complimented you on, I know I can. I think that subconsciously these items become our favourites. We often wear them more frequently and they can influence future purchases.

Buying clothes that make us feel good is important, and when others agree by way of a compliment, it positively reinforces that the choices we made, regarding style, colour, and shape were valid.

If I am walking down the street or am out in a bar or restaurant and I spot a woman whose outfit I adore, and think that she looks amazing, I always make the effort to complement her.

"

Excuse me I think your shoes or dress are beautiful.

I think your outfit is fabulous on you.

It takes so little effort on my behalf, and if I truly believe that something looks amazing on someone, then why not tell her, and make her smile. It costs nothing and the feel-good effect is priceless.

While writing this chapter I couldn't but help reminisce about some of my early style choices. There have been so many!

Let's start with my shell suit. I'm from Liverpool after all, how could I write a book on style and not mention that iconic piece? I was about eight years old when I got my first one, (many more followed). We were going to France on holiday and my dad took my sister and I to the market and bought us both one, thankfully not matching. Mine was turquoise with yellow and white panels and, if memory serves me correctly, my younger sisters was lilac with pink panels – luckily there appears to be no photographic evidence in existence!

As a fan of the 1980s boy band Bros, I was quick to adopt the 'Brosette' uniform that included, white T shirt, ripped jeans and boots with bottle tops attached to the laces.

When I hit my early teens, I proudly wore Body Shop T shirts denouncing animal testing (shockingly, 30 years on, it is still happening in some parts of the world) and became a temporary vegetarian. I also experimented with the goth look and at the height of Spice-mania, dyed my hair like Geri Halliwell's and dressed as a Spice Girl, spandex galore. I know, I was such a teenage cliché!

Despite all the cringeworthy looks there is one item from my youth that I still look back on with fondness. In the early 1990's I saved up £92 (nuts!!) for a pair of Nike Air Max. There'd not been anything like them before.

They were almost space age with an air bubble in the heel. For months I'd walk past them in the window of the local sports shop, hoping they would still be there when I had saved up enough money. In the end, I sold my clarinet to pay for them! Early warning of my future shoe addiction! I adored those trainers and wore them until I could no more.

Until I bought my first pair of Louboutin heels, those Nikes were the shoes I had coveted the most in my whole life! The point of that story is to demonstrate that when you save up or sacrifice something to buy an item, then you really must want it. As a result, you will love it and wear it for years and that really is the essence of sustainable style.

I adore getting dressed up. There are few better feelings than wearing your favourite clothes, donning a high heel, putting on make-up, and having your hair done. That level of glamour is wonderful but, for most of us, simply not practical every day. I seldom wake up and put on any old thing. Some things are chosen for comfort, or because I love them, or to portray a certain look, or even as a nod to nostalgia, but I make a conscious decision about every item I wear, and I want you to do that too.

Selfie Files

How annoying is it when you know you nailed a look but can't quite remember exactly what it was? Simple solution – snap a selfie and no I am not talking about the whole Instagram #ootd or even a public post anywhere on social media rather, just a private photo, as a reminder of what you wore when and how. You can create a file on your phone and dump them all there, added bonus you can keep track of what you wore to where, as well as it being an instant inspiration with a dash of confidence and the feel-good factor. You'll remember that dress/shoe/belt combo forever.

Only wear your favourite clothes on days ***ending in 'y'***

SHERYL BOLDEN

Life can be hard,
getting dressed
should be ***easy***

8

How to *edit your wardrobe*

Hands up if you have you stood in front of your open wardrobe flicking through the bulging contents while silently screaming,

I have nothing to wear

You too, I thought so! In fact, I'm not sure I've ever met a woman who hasn't.

Friends, colleagues, clients and pretty much every other female I've ever met, have told me that this is their biggest fashion frustration.

In fact, back in 2013, I'd gotten so tired of hearing the same complaint, especially from women who literally had the wardrobe of my dreams, that I founded Make My Wardrobe Work.

A wardrobe editing service designed to combat the "I have nothing to wear" syndrome. I spent time with women in the comfort and security of their own home editing and reworking the clothes they already owned leaving them with a wardrobe full of clothes they always want to wear. Now, I am going to teach you how to successfully edit your own wardrobe, yourself.

Before I get into the 'How To', I think it's important I share with you 'The Why' Why should you edit your clothes, what is the upside?

To answer that let me explain the three principles upon which any good wardrobe is based.

1. **If you can't see it,** you can't wear it
2. **If you don't love it,** you won't wear it
3. **If you can't style it,** you can't maximise it

Think back to chapter two, where I talked about only buying clothes that you really love? Well, I like to think of that as the equivalent of a retail buyer selecting the right stock for the right store. If your wardrobe is your favourite shop, and you don't love the clothes it sells, or if they don't fit or suit your lifestyle, then the chances are high that you will metaphorically walk into your shop and leave empty handed. You will probably still be in your underwear, frustrated and irate as you reluctantly return and put on the same old thing, that you don't even like, while simultaneously juggling the morning chaos. Finally, you leave the house – late and feeling uninspired by your sartorial selection!

This is why an edit is important, it ensures you know, love and wear what you own to ultimately make your own life easier.

Before you start your edit, remember that each item you own should earn its place in your wardrobe. Think of your wardrobe like an exclusive private members club – only the best or the most useful are admitted.

During an edit, the question I was asked most frequently was "*do you like it?*" and my answer would be the same every time, "*it is irrelevant what I like, I am not wearing it*". I would remind clients of their three chosen words that they wanted people to use to describe them – based only on their clothes. Common answers would include stylish, pulled together, approachable, professional, fun, classy and so on. I would then honestly assess if said item reflected the chosen words and we'd go from there. Clothes are subjective and that is a good thing. No one person's personal taste is more valid than another's.

Right, now on to the all-important 'How To'.

You'll need to make time and space to do it properly, "*do it once and do it well*" as my late Nana used to say. Other than time and space, you will need a full-length mirror, some pins, three boxes or large bags, a phone for taking photos is handy, forget the vino you'll just get all misty eyed and nostalgic and never want to get rid of anything or despair at how much money you have wasted over the years, neither are conducive to a successful edit. Friends are optional but choose wisely. It needs to be someone who you trust to tell you the truth (tactfully) but also someone who understands what works for you, not just what they like.

A 2018 study, commissioned in the UK by Ariel, revealed that the average British woman spends in excess of a thousand pounds per year, owns 95 pieces of clothing but only wears 59% of them regularly. It is clear that our wardrobes are not working hard enough!

Before you begin to actually edit, let me contextualise why this is and how most people's clothes are split, generally speaking, there are five categories.

1 Always Wear

This is the infamous 20% of your wardrobe that regularly gets an outing – the dependable everyday pieces, aka your trusty staples! It is likely you love these pieces and they score highly on your 'Sheryl' scale. They seldom let you down but it's easy to get bored of them. These should be easy to access but don't be afraid to mix them up and wear them in different ways.

2 Have to Wear

These are essential clothes that seldom get us excited, but we can't live without them. Think gym gear, sleepwear, warm weather essentials and those comfy pieces that you just want to pull on when you get home – the key with these is not to clutter up limited hanging space, so store them in drawers and boxes and don't keep too many of them. Let them go when they become so bad that even opening the door to the postman would be embarrassing.

3 Hardly Wear

This could be due to lifestyle. Living in Hong Kong, these are the clothes that I miss the most. So many of my London favourites fall into this category: trench coat, wool coat, and chunky knitwear. If you look after your clothes, they will last a lifetime – so let them. Don't get rid of something you adore just because you don't wear it very often. If space is at a premium then think about storing them away from your main wardrobe.

4 Was going to wear

I hate to say it but these are more likely to be shopping mistakes. Clothes that seemed so alluring in the shop, but when you got it home it didn't quite have the same wow factor. If every time you try it on, you end up wearing something else, then the chances are that it's the wrong colour or wrong shape for you. As frustrating as a failed purchase is, there are options. Think about alteration, restyling and even selling.

5 Wish I could wear

I have yet to meet a person who doesn't have a few of these items in their wardrobe! Usually, it's because the item doesn't fit, so ask yourself question, if it did fit then would you wear it? If the answer is no, then the solution is easy – donate it, swap it, or sell it. However, if you truly can't bear to prematurely let go of something you love, then take it out of the wardrobe and pack it away and revisit if your body shape changes. There's nothing more frustrating than looking at clothes you love but can't wear.

A good friend of mine recently lost a significant amount of weight. Other than feeling much healthier she was so delighted when she uncovered two vacuum packed bags full of clothes that she had not worn since her first pregnancy, eight years previously. The delight at getting a whole 'new' wardrobe that she still loved, was inspiring and reminded me to always keep those pieces I would regret not owning.

As a side note on this topic, I know people who do everything they can to squeeze into a particular size, refusing to move up a size even if it looks more flattering.

My advice is, ignore the label! If it fits well, wear it. Who cares what the number on the label says, you can always cut it out!

To know what you are working with, it is best to start from the very beginning. Take everything out, and I mean everything; shoes, gym kit, PJ's, accessories, bags the whole lot.

Everything you want to keep will go back into the wardrobe but the items you no longer love will fall into three areas, so set up your boxes or bags into Donate, Sell/Swap and Tailor.

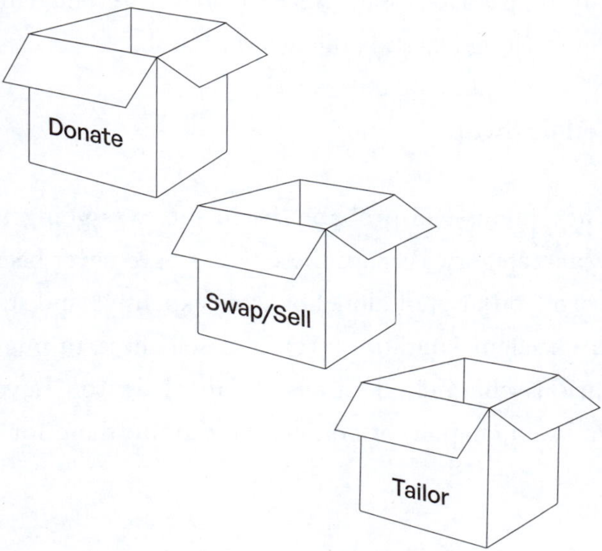

Donate

Please, only ever include items that are in good condition, no stains, mould, holes, nor rips. If you are donating these to someone in need then please give them something they would be proud to wear, and that you would pass to them in person. It is probable their circumstances are bad enough without having your old worn-out clothes bestowed upon them. You can also donate to friends and family! Perhaps you think that gorgeous top would look so much better and be worn so much more by your sister then yourself!

Go on be selfless. Pass it over. My sister has been a grateful recipient over the years, in fact I bet her wardrobe is a lot less full since Covid has prevented me from visiting her and adding to her stash.

Sell or Swap

These items will probably be in the 'was going to wear' category. Perhaps these pieces have never been worn (you are not alone) or were expensive and still in excellent condition. You can sell these through various channels. I discuss them all in the Love, Preloved chapter, or you can hold on to them for a swap party. Either option is a great way to claw back some of your investment.

Tailoring

So underrated! If you can make a small change that results in a longer life cycle for your clothes, improves it's cost per wear and means you will wear it better, then absolutely make the change. It's one of the most sustainable ways you can make your wardrobe work.

Now for decision time. Before deciding if something stays or goes, revert to chapter two, The Art of Investing. Pretend you are in a changing room and all your clothes are there to be bought, would you buy it again?

If the answer is yes, bingo! Put it back in the wardrobe and move on. For those items that you love but perhaps feel you have worn a lot, don't hesitate to archive them so you don't get too bored, then re-introduce them after a period of hibernation, I bet you'll love them like an old friend, you can continue to make new memories wearing them – not to mention further improving their cost per wear!

If you think no, then add it to the relevant box and move on. The chances are that the items you would buy again score a four or a five, from the earlier Sheryl's Score Chart. The items you didn't hesitate to say goodbye to probably rank as a one or a two.

That leaves us with the not sures, normally the threes. Worry not, these pieces are not always lost causes! If you are leaning towards liking it but knowing that the fit is just not quite right, this could be solved with a bit of tweaking here and there. It really can make all the difference. A long sleeve may be more flattering as a three quarter, drawing the eye to your waist, often our narrowest point, rather than our hips, often the widest. The length of a skirt or dress can be critical and an inch or two really does matter. Alternatively, the colour may not be right and so overdying could be an option.

I have done this a few times and it works better on light colours and natural fabrics. But a word of warning if the stitching or a zip for example is visible you may end up with a contrast as these are usually polyester which won't absorb the dye in the same way cotton does.

Another reason for the low score could be that it was once a lovely dress that you wore to special occasions but now you would choose something else and you feel a bit flat about it. This is the time to change its end use.

Like I talked about in the chapter one, Cost Per Wear, change the way you think of that dress. Instead of it being 'special' wear it as an elevated everywhere dress, you'll suddenly see that fancy blouse that was for dinner it in a different light when you pair it with jeans for the school pick up or work.

As they say, 'Love Conquers All' and we have established that you should only keep the clothes you really love to wear in your wardrobe. But what about those sentimental pieces, the dress from your school prom, your engagement party, your first interview, your milestone birthdays, and countless other occasions that you feel love and nostalgia towards? No matter what, if it has meaning and you love it but won't wear it then never get rid of it. I'm thinking of a particular black leather mini dress – last seen around 2011, I'm too old, it's too short but there is no way I am getting rid of it. It's still a beautiful item that I look forward to passing to my daughter, in fact she'll be overflowing in what will then be considered vintage, my old clothes from the 1990's and beyond. Store these out of your wardrobe. Ideally in acetate free tissue, vacuum packed or even if particularly special with a third-party specialist.

I have been fortunate to have worn many of my mum's clothes from the late 1970's to parties in the

2000s. I still wear my late Granny's old faux fur coat, and one of my biggest regrets, is that I did not keep and alter some items that belonged to my Nana before she passed.

Now you know what you are keeping it's time to put the clothes away! There are more ways to organise your wardrobe than clothes to fit in it. Some people like to organise by product type, so all the skirts are hung together, dresses together etc. Some by 'end use' that is all the party clothes together, the workwear together, casual clothes together, beachwear together and so on. Some people like to hang by colour – although I find this a bit pointless rarely do you wake up thinking today I must wear black. It is much more likely you would say today I am going to work and so flicking through kaftans and sequin skirts – even if they are all black, is largely unhelpful!

End use is very popular but I would caution that in organising this way it often results in your clothes being put into metaphorical boxes and so there is a tendency that something can only be worn to a certain place, – but more on that later. On balance, my preference is to separate by product type. You can then sub organise e.g., tops are then hung by colour or sleeve length or end use.

For many of us, our storage comprises varying combinations of wardrobes, shelves, and drawers, and sometime also split across different rooms. I wish this book came with a complimentary walk-in wardrobe and an instruction manual on how to fill it but sadly not!

Of course, if you have the time, space, and money for a full-blown Carrie Bradshaw wardrobe renovation, go for it. But the reality is most of us don't so we have to be creative and make the most of what we have, whether that be an excess of vertical storage space, built-in shelving, or multiple hanging rods, to our advantage. In all instances Google and Pinterest are your friend.

Like most things in life, I highly recommend organising your clothes in a way that works best for you. Here are some important tips that you should follow.

- **Hang as much as you can.** It is easier to see what you have when it is hung. When space is limited make room by not hanging activewear, sleepwear, beachwear (except fancy kaftans and dresses) and denim.

- **Never ever hang knitwear.** The weight of the yarn and the construction means it literally grows on a hanger, so after a while it will be longer than intended and all out of shape, especially on the shoulder where the hanger leads to distortion.

- **Roll don't fold.** When T shirts, vests, jersey shorts, and such like live in a drawer, it's much better to roll them and place side by side rather than to lay them flat on top of each other. By piling high you will forget what is there and then never wear the ones at the bottom of the pile.

- **Hang inside out** those pieces that are delicate to avoid snagging and incidental damage.

- **Drawer Dividers.** These are so handy, especially for underwear, swimwear, activewear, and nightwear. We don't normally have enough space to dedicate a whole drawer to each of these categories. Using dividers can help organise those drawers that can easily become chaotic.

- **Maximise the vertical space.** This means walls, top shelves, doors, and even that dead space between the floor and the hems of your hanging dresses. All of this can be effectively used, especially when it comes to accessories.

- **Don't forget Accessories.** From experience, shoes, bags, scarves, jewellery and so on are frequently hidden and subsequently forgotten. If you can't see them, you won't wear them – says the broken record!

Your wardrobe should be your ***favourite boutique***

SHERYL BOLDEN

9

Shopping *Your Wardrobe*

Your wardrobe should be your favourite boutique. This is one of my most used phrases and now that you have completed your edit, it really should be. Think of your wardrobe as a shop where you really love everything on sale, a shop in which every item not only fits you but also and looks great, and also a shop where you don't need to pay for the clothes!

Sometimes, having a great selection of clothes isn't enough. To create a wardrobe that you really want to 'shop' time and time again, aesthetically it needs to inspire you too. Everyone wants to open their wardrobe, no matter how small, and feel excited. You should love and want to wear each item as much now as on the day you bought it. (And, if you didn't love it then, it begs the questions, why did you buy it?).

Your shop must make choosing an outfit easy and this is where presentation is key. I have been dreaming of a walk-in wardrobe for as long as I knew they existed. My long-suffering husband is sick of me endlessly designing, mentally decorating and filling this imaginary room, that I will one day create. But back to reality.

A walk-in wardrobe is a luxury that few of us have, especially living here in Hong Kong where space is at such a premium that a wardrobe with hanging space and two doors is a bonus. No matter how small the space, there are things you can do to ensure it is inviting and practical, as well as inspiring.

Merchandise it well.

As I stressed in the previous chapter, if you can't see it, you can't wear it! One of the top three reasons for not wearing something is forgetting you own it! (The other two are, it doesn't fit and I don't like it- on me, but I've more than covered those points already!) A cluttered and squashed wardrobe is not only overwhelming but it prevents you rotating and as a result you go back to the same few things time and time again. There have been countless times I have found items at the back of drawers or laid in a heap, at the bottom of the wardrobe and thought, "*oh I love that, totally forgot I had it. Damn, it would have been great with that skirt I wore last Saturday*".

Stock the essentials.

Every wardrobe should have a collection of great quality basics that are the foundation of any outfit. These vary from person to person depending on their style and lifestyle and what suits them but common pieces in this category include, a classic shirt, great jeans, a well-fitting blazer, an elevated T shirt, a dress that fits you like a glove, and a neutral cashmere jumper. It is important to work on what the best versions of these are for you, from colour to the shape and cut, there is seldom a one shape suits all. These pieces can be mixed and matched and are versatile and timeless.

Owning these sartorial building blocks make it much easier to outfit build. "*What is outfit building?*" I hear you ask. Well, it's the way we create an outfit, usually starting with the focal point, this could be anything from a quirky item that is just 'you' or a sentimental piece that makes you smile. An accessory can also be the hero piece of your look. When you have decided upon that, you begin to construct the rest of the outfit around it. While I'm a big fan of having an array of unique and vintage finds in eclectic colours and prints to outfit build around, a wardrobe filled only with these becomes very difficult to wear, because nothing really goes. Never forget to include a level of comfort if the outfit needs to be worn all day!

Make sure everything in your wardrobe is 'fit for sale'

What I mean by this, is if your wardrobe was an actual shop, you could put any item on and walk out wearing it. After all, the point of having clothes in the wardrobe is to wear them. You'd be surprised at how many times in the past I've congratulated myself on how easy it was to find the perfect choice only to discover it's ripped, or there's a stain, a button missing or it's not ironed. I know, I know don't shout, this is divisive and I see both sides of the argument. Ironing on a need to basis has its merits, but for me, I want it to look nice hanging up and I am always running late so I'm in the ironed then away camp – but each to their own.

Hanger Appeal

Good coat hangers are key for a few reasons. Aesthetically your clothing will look more inviting, creating a boutique feel, if there is uniformity – that term hanger appeal – yep it means something! The right hanger will keep your clothes in better condition. The type of hanger you use depends on personal preference, and space. Wooden ones look great – literal hanger appeal and the advantage of the bulkier design gives your clothes more room to breathe, keeping them wrinkle free for longer. The downside is that they take up valuable wardrobe space and cost more – this is an investment hanger. Slim ones with a velvet style coating are perfect because they allow you to maximise space, and the soft round shape won't dent your clothes and they work for many product types and the coating ensures clothes don't slip off. No matter what type you go for avoid the metal wire hangers. They will deform and ultimately damage your clothes.

Smell

We all have our favourite smells, adding these to wardrobes and drawers can really make a difference. I love it when my clothes smell great, even if it's just a nostalgic laundry powder. I love it even more when I have a luxury scent hanging in the wardrobe kind of like a fancy version of a car air freshener. Other than scented drawer liners (they don't have to be the type that Aunt Ethel bought you for Christmas ten years ago) you could also add a little bowl in the base of the wardrobe filled with pou pouri or place an infuser. Strongly scented soaps wrapped in thin fabric, to protect your clothing from the soap, can share their fragrance with the rest of your wardrobe.

Organisation

I'm a planner, I like to know what I am wearing in advance. Rarely will I randomly decide on an outfit on the day. But my recent research showed that I was in the minority. Less than 15% of women I asked, planned what they were going to wear before each day. Meaning that over 85% decided on the morning – who has the time? No wonder so many said they threw on the first thing that was clean and fitted.

Now I am not suggesting you start by planning all seven days in advance. Start slowly and give it a go one night when you have an extra ten minutes to pull out something you have not worn for ages. Take a bit of time to think about how you can style it and add it to your weekly rotation then, it's like having a bonus new outfit because it's been hanging untouched for so long. Having this little bit of time allows you to add some interesting accessories and shoes that are often elusive at 7am. Most women I know say they wished they accessorized more.

Wear More Ways

Do you compartmentalize your clothes into work wear, holiday pieces, weekend clothes, going out clothes and rarely shall they mix? If so, (and you are definitely not alone,) then the biggest way to maximise your wardrobe and get the most out of your 'shop' is to think of it like a breakfast buffet, - yes, we are back to food again!

There is no rule to say you have to have cereal and eggs for breakfast, if the noodles and dim sum are there, then go ahead, if it's what you want. So, in the same way, there is no rule to say a particular dress is only for parties, or that a certain blouse shouldn't be seen out of working hours. The next time you see something in your wardrobe that you want to wear more often, ask yourself, why not? The top didn't tell you it was only to be worn only to work or the skirt only contracted to the weekend? Your clothes can't talk, they don't have feelings or an agenda and it is up to you to decide how and when you wear them. So be brave and wear more ways. Don't be afraid to take that silk print blouse that usually goes with the suit and team it with a leather skirt and heels for dinner. Go even further, wear it with shorts and sandals to weekend brunch. Buying something you can only wear with one other thing in your wardrobe is a false economy and it'll never return a low cost per wear.

Always Accessorize

Make sure your shop has an accessories department. A scarf with a flash of colour, an unusual shoe, the statement bracelet: these are the pieces that inject personality, style, and individuality to your outfit. But to realistically ensure you include these pieces, they need to be visible. Put your shoes on racks or stick photos onto their boxes. Take out your jewellery and invest in organizers to hang it where you'll see it. Belts can be great for creating a waist and adding a flash of colour, whilst making a look appear chic. For me, accessories are more than the cherry on the sartorial cake, they are the glue that holds your outfit together.

And finally, whichever outfit you choose, make sure you love it. I always find when I add in an extra special piece, it could be sentimental, a gift from a loved one or something I have saved hard for, I love it that little extra bit more.

Style is ***not a display of wealth*** *but an* ***expression of imagination***

10

Looking Good *for Less*

One of the biggest myths in fashion is that it costs a lot of money to look good. The truth that every marketing agency and retailer doesn't want to you know is that it really doesn't have to. For decades, Fast Fashion brands have been selling us a dream of designer dresses for a fraction of the price. It doesn't matter how many 'splurge or save' articles magazines throw at us, the reality is, being dressed head to toe in cheap, poorly made clothes seldom looks chic or expensive.

But you can elevate your look for less and here's how

1 Wear well-fitting clothes

Nothing looks as cheap as clothes that don't fit. Too big looks shoddy and too small looks crass. Buttons bursting open, trousers that bunch up at the ankles and sleeves that are too long, do not scream Saville Row. Hems should sit just right, wherever that is on you. A little alteration to some High Street tailoring can really make a difference and give the illusion of made to measure.

2 Never underestimate underwear

Never underestimate the importance of good underwear. It can literally change your shape. It is worth getting properly fitted for a bra, it has the power to transform your outfit, and your silhouette. Buy the best you can and wash it carefully.

The power of knickers is not to be laughed at. Choose well, from my experience, comfort is king. Come on, I can't be the only one who has walked around all day wishing I'd picked out a different pair! As for black pants showing through a light-coloured skirt, well it just looks a little naff, don't you think?

3 Make the basics count

Invest well in classic pieces, those staples that you will wear again and again. Be careful when buying black, in some synthetic fibres it can look shiny and cheap.

The better the cut, the more luxe it will look, so consider buying more premium brands, either preloved, in the sale or at an outlet, where you are likely to get the most bang for your buck. Take the time to find the perfect jeans for you, you won't regret it. These sartorial building blocks are the pieces to be strategic about, quality over quantity, always. If invested in and worn right, they will give you a fantastic cost per wear.

4 Best Foot Forward

When you want to look a million dollars, don't forget your feet. Shoes should be in good condition, polished and well heeled. Same could be said of your feet if that is what is on show. Nothing ruins an outfit quite like a bad shoe. Often one of the most loved but least looked after purchases. Get to know your cobbler, repairing a well-fitting shoe will save you money in the long run and is far more sustainable than buying multiple cheap pairs that could quickly end up in landfill.

Black shoes with bare legs can detract away from the outfit, great if you want to show off those four-inch sexy stilettos but can put a damper on a great outfit. Nudes and neutrals are a posh girls staple and there is nothing quite like a statement shoe – personally speaking my favourite way to give a subtle (or not so) twist to a simple outfit.

5 Invest in good bag

Please do not translate as “buy a designer bag” (I will openly admit this is my weakness) I love a lovely bag! But a lovely bag does not have to carry a designer logo. A good bag should work for your lifestyle – for some that will be big enough to carry the kitchen sink, stylishly, and for others it will carry only the essentials. The bag should be good quality, well made, versatile and timeless. Five years ago, I probably would have said it should be leather, but with the advances in vegan materials I no longer think it the case. These days it can be difficult to tell if it’s leather or not, I’ve stood in a shop and had to have a good sniff, and then read the label just to be absolutely sure.

Always avoid cheap ‘copy copy’ rip offs.

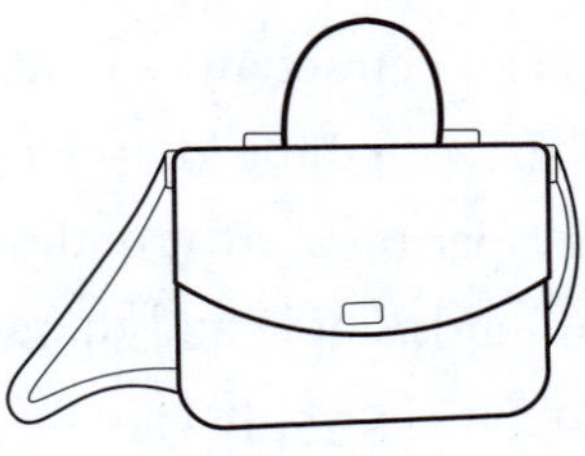

In a world full of trends,
I want to remain a classic.

6 The devils in the detail

Usually, it is the most subtle details that elevate an outfit. Roll up the sleeves of your shirt or tuck in your t-shirt. Cuff your jeans and add an unexpected splash of colour. Add a belt where appropriate, not only can it be flattering, but it can also give that air of pulled togetherness, especially when there are belt loops. These little extras show that you know what you're doing and can radiate an effortlessness chicness that money can't buy.

7 Too much of something is never good

Young celebs and models aside (even then it's questionable) very few people can carry off a single trend head to toe. Often it looks a bit too try hard or worse. It says to the world that you are devoid of your own style. Instead, if you want to create a fashion forward look that is a bit classier, I'd advise mixing some statement trend pieces, colours, or accessories with classic outfit builders to anchor your look. Don't be afraid of wearing skirts or trousers in bold colours or prints. It can look striking and powerful, especially when the rest of the outfit is paired back and classic.

8 Good grooming

Nothing shouts cheap like a chipped nail or unbrushed hair. Stains, missing buttons, falling down hems don't shout out chic either. Own a lint brush to manage stray hairs and fluff and a pair of snippers for removing loose threads and keep a small bottle of nail varnish remover and a file to hand. It doesn't cost a lot of money to ensure the simple things are done, as my late Nana used to say, "*take pride in your appearance, no excuses for sloppiness*"

Trendy is the ***last stage before tacky***

KARL LAGERFELD

If it's ***worth wearing****, it's* ***worth repairing****.*

11

Caring for your clothes

It goes without saying that if you want to get the best out of anything you need to look after it. If you bought a bike, for example, I'm sure you'd make sure the tyres were pumped up and the chain oiled and by keeping it out of the rain so it didn't get rusty, it would be good to go every time you needed it. Now, apply that same logic to your clothes. You have invested time and money filling your wardrobe with these clothes, ones you really want to wear. By treasuring them and treating them with love and care, they will be there for you whenever you need to wear them.

An easy way to help keep our clothes newer for longer, is to look after them. It sounds simple but you would be surprised how many people don't. To ensure that those sartorial investments give you the best and most sustainable return, follow my trusty tips.

1 Fix them

I know it seems like a pain at the time but when you notice a small rip, or a button pops off or a hem hangs down, fix it as soon as you can. If you don't want to or can't then outsource it. If you don't fix it, you can't wear it and a wardrobe full of unwearable clothes is not sustainable.

2 Put them away

As tempting as it can be after a long day (or night!), to leave your clothes where you took them off, this is not helpful. Your clothes do not live on the floor, or over the back of a chair, or on the bathroom rail. If they don't need to be washed, they should be hung or folded and put away as soon as you have taken them off. If a little creased, hanging them in the bathroom can help to get rid of the wrinkles and prevent you having to re iron – saving time and energy. If you have not sweated and they are not visibly dirty you don't always need to wash them, hanging them to air and refresh naturally for a few hours can be just as effective.

3 Wash them less

Typically, we all wash our clothes more than needed. Aside from the environmental damage caused by overusing the washer and dryer as well as the release of microplastics through the washing process, too much washing can be damaging to our clothes. The colour can fade, the fabric can pill, and the seams can spiral, especially in T-shirts. Obviously, some clothes such as underwear, active wear, sleepwear, and those worn close to your body when sweating need to be washed frequently. But jeans, sweaters and often skirts, suiting and dresses are over washed when an airing would suffice.

When washing by machine many retailers now advocate washing at 30 degrees. According research carried out by Ariel, this reduces the energy used to run the machine and saves up to 57% on running costs when compared to washing at 40°C. A liquid detergent is smoother than the powdered alterative which creates more friction between the clothes and, according to Prof Andrew Groves, head of the fashion design course at the University of Westminster, it is the friction that removes the dirt but it is also responsible for releasing more fibres, while also distorting a garment's shape and colour. The fewer clothes you place in the drum, the less friction is created.

Be careful when washing delicate items like bras. Machine washing can destroy fabrics such as lace or silks, it can also make the wires pop out, the colours fade, and if your bra has a moulded cup, machine washing can also make it go all misshapen. It is better to handwash but I'm a realist and I know this is not always practical. So when you do machine wash, always do up the hook and eyes to stop any snagging, use a lingerie bag, and wash on a low temperature. Reshape when it's out and hang it to dry or lie it on a flat surface, and please never, ever, tumble dry.

4 Know your labels

No, not the designer ones! Far more important than the brand label is the wash care label. It's legally required, usually white and filled with symbols and instructions. It must be sewn into every garment so as a consumer, you understand how best to care for your new acquisition. Deciphering these symbols is key to prolonging your piece.

I will never forget how annoyed (at myself) I was when not long after leaving home, and now doing my own washing, I put a beautiful wool jumper in the washing machine. When I took it out, I was devastated to see the only person it would fit would be a five-year old. I was gutted, it was a harsh lesson to learn. From that point onwards, I read up on how to wash certain fabrics and yarns, I didn't want to make that mistake but dry cleaning was an expense I couldn't always afford.

Some fibres are more robust than others, typically manmade synthetics like polyester and nylon can be washed with ease while natural fibres such as silk and wool must be handled with extra care. By understanding more, you can make informed decisions on how you care for your clothes.

TIP: Before cutting out any oversized care label, familiarise yourself with the information, maybe take a photo and a note of the item for future washing.

5 To dry clean or not, dry clean...

Dry cleaning is expensive and it's a chemical process, so should be used sparingly. It'll come as no surprise that retailers can be over cautious when recommending dry cleaning. Often it's not necessary, a delicate hand wash in cool water would be more helpful to your wallet and the environment but concerned that the interpretation of cool or delicate is subjective, the use of the dry clean symbol is the retailers get out of jail card.

While I am not advocating that everything can be hand washed, (I wouldn't hand wash a wool coat!) I do believe by that understanding a little more about the fibres and by taking the time to wash accordingly, with care, you can reduce your dependence on dry cleaning.

Advances in washing machine technology have resulted in much more sophisticated programmes which are kinder to clothes. Use laundry bags for delicate and embellished items and always when handwashing, be careful the water it not too hot. It is the heat that often ruins fibres not the water itself. If dry cleaning is necessary then look for one that is more environmentally conscious and offers biodegradable and health friendly detergents.

6 Keep stains free

As someone who is clumsier than most, there is very little I have not inadvertently poured down a dress, from obvious red wine incidents to gravy during Sunday lunch. But my worst attempt at ruining something I loved was during work trip. I'd just purchased a beautiful ochre silk dress, it was having its first outing, to a presentation that I'd flown half the way around the world to attend, when I accidently spilt the contents of a black fountain pen all over myself! Saving that was definitely one of my biggest sartorial successes to date.

The key is to remedy stains quickly, but to do that you need to know what removes a certain type of stain and get access to it pronto. What you treat each type of stain with can determine if it can be cured or if it's terminal. Always pre-treat the stain before chucking it in the washing machine.

Red Wine

Cover with salt or baking soda, then blot.

Coffee

Blot, then dab with a mix of warm water, dish soap, and white vinegar.

Oil/Grease

Cover with baking soda, baby powder, or cornstarch to soak up the grease.

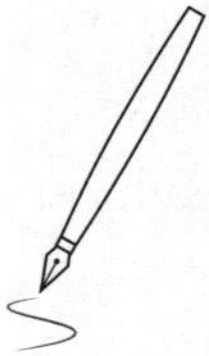

Ink

Apply white toothpaste, then rub vigorously with fabric.

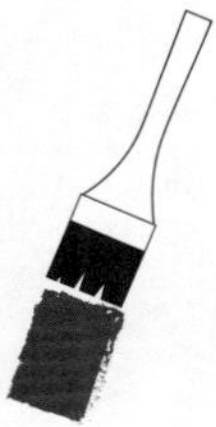

Paint

Dab with paint thinner, rinse, treat with a stain remover, then launder.

Blood

Soak the stain in a mixture of vinegar and warm water, then dab.

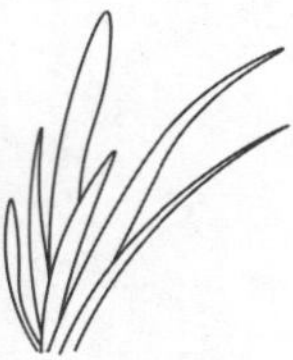

Grass

Mix baking soda with hydrogen peroxide and a few drops of dish soap. Soak for a few hours.

Deodorant

Soak in white vinegar for up to an hour, scrub, then launder.

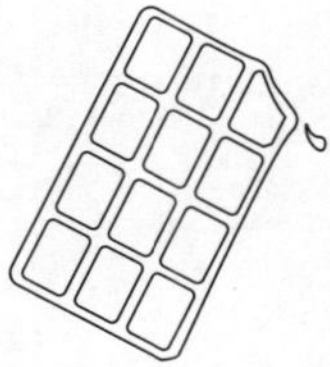

Chocolate

Cover with laundry detergent for 10 minutes, then soak in cold water before laundering.

PART 3

Shopping

BEWARE of the Sale

12

Sales, *Glorious* Sales

It draws you in, pulling you through the shop doors like a magnet. Pulse racing upon the sight - rows upon rows of rails, rammed with hangers full of cut-price clothes, their oversized price labels flapping in the air con. Fellow shoppers cajoling and competing for the loot, barging against you to join the mile long till queue. You get home excited, spill contents of the bag. Despair hits. None of it fits or looks good. Moths to the flame, we are slaves to the sale!

There is something about huge red SALE signs that turns even the most prudent of shoppers into a shopaholic. Friends of mine who usually like to browse and compare styles before buying have been known to run a mock, rummaging, barging, and even hoarding everything insight, then handing over a credit card quicker than you can say, “bargain”

Others, who are normally rational and considered spenders set their alarm clock on Christmas night to get up at some ungodly hour the following day. They drive, in the dark, to an out-of-town mall and queue up to enter a famous High Street brand's Boxing Day sale. I'd understand if they were going the extra mile for a designer handbag, or a pair of jeans or trainers that would normally be out of budget but all that effort to save five or ten pounds on something they could more than afford full price is baffling. It shows just how impactful the marketing of the sale can be.

Now don't get me wrong, I'm not against sales, some of the best items I own were bought in a sale and for me going to the sales also evokes nostalgia and happy memories. Especially of my teenage years when my friends and I would hop on the train to Liverpool and head to the shops, armed with vouchers and money gifted to us for Christmas. We loved to pour over the sale rails. Sweaters from NAF NAF, bags from Benetton and something that would make us look older than we really were from Morgan or Miss Sixty! Those are some blasts from the past!

But the thought of sale shopping also evokes frustration and annoyance at the amount of money that I, and many of the women I have worked with have wasted over the years.

> *A bargain is something you* ***don't need*** *at a price you can't resist*
>
> FRANKLIN JONES

I'm sure you too have bought something in a sale, thinking you had gotten a great deal only to find it months later unworn because you don't really love it, or it doesn't fit. In almost every single wardrobe I have edited there is at least one item with the tags still on. When asked why it hadn't been worn, more often than not, the answer was, "*I don't really like it, I bought it in the sale*".

The dictionary definition of bargain is:

> *A thing bought or offered for sale much more cheaply than is usual or expected*

But when is a bargain really saving you money and when is it wasting money?

In simple terms the answer is, you save money only when you purchase something for less, that you were going to buy regardless.

An alternative type of bargain that doesn't literally save you money, but it's my favourite kind all the same, is when you fall in love with something which was perfect, save for the price, so you walked away, only to then spot it in the right colour and the right size in the sale! Now that is a bargain to behold. There is no purchase quite as satisfying.

I grew up believing a bargain was a wonderful thing and it can be, but over the years I have learnt to identify when the store is having the last laugh. The reasons why you, me, and millions of others waste money in the sales are numerous, but to assure you that you are not alone here are some of my favourite quotes from friends and clients alike, I hope they don't sound too familiar!

- I really needed the other size but it was sold out, I thought if I bought it, I'd lose weight...

- I just loved the print so much. I thought I might make it into something else.

- It was so fashionable and everyone had one but when I tried it on at home, I realised I just looked ridiculous.

- I loved it in blue but they only had green, it was so cheap I bought it anyway.

It was only a couple of pounds, it seemed criminal not to buy it, I'll find someone to give it to"

It was buy one, get one half price – they were almost giving it away!"

I'd be lying if I told you that I had never stood in front of the sale rail and been swayed to spend on something I didn't really need, just because the perceived saving was so big that it was impossible for me walk away. Returning home and trying to convince my husband that I '*had*' to buy a fabulous new wool coat in June, when we'd run out of storage space and live in a country with an average winter temperature of 19 degrees was not easy! My defence, "*how could I possibly not buy it when it should have been over £200 and I only paid £50*"

The only thing better than buying something you really love, is buying something you really love for less! To bag a bargain like that, you need to do your homework. Here are my top tips for succeeding at the sales.

- Make a list of the things you really want and where they are from.
- Sign up to those retailers' newsletters, often they email the sale details first.
- Know which branch had sufficient stock of your favourite pieces, then ask the sales team when their sale starts, then go on the first day.
- Put the item in your online check out basket, sometimes the price reduction is automatically applied when the sales go live allowing you a speedy purchase before it sells out.
- Consider buying less exciting but equally necessary items such as underwear and active wear on sale. Either saving money or upgrading to a brand you would not normally spend so much on.
- Purchase presents in advance (just remember you have bought them!)

It's also worth remembering, next time you're hunting for your most coveted item, that often the big branches sell out of more fashionable or popular styles quicker than smaller regional stores. Not quite a sale story, but back in about 2004 a fast fashion retailer and a famous fashion magazine created a capsule collection and there was this one dress that I'd seen in the magazine and I wanted it soooo much, it was just perfect. I queued at Oxford Street and when I got to the front it was gone. I tried all the main London stores to no avail. That weekend we were visiting my in-laws in Essex and we stopped by Lakeside and to my amazement there was a whole rack of them! The dress was linen and lovely and I am still wearing it to this day, the cost per wear must be in the minus by now!

The reason a retailer reduces something is because they have too much stock. This can be for a whole variety of reasons; they bought too much, the colour wasn't how it was supposed to be, there was a mistake in the pattern and the fit isn't right, the product arrived later than agreed and so the opportunity to sell was reduced – the list is endless. All brands account for a certain level of stock being sold at a reduced margin in the sale, but for any brand, too much overstock can be a problem that must be cleared before it becomes a financial and ethical issue.

Have you ever wondered why some items have big reductions and others are barely reduced? To explain, a quick lesson in 'sell through' a retailing term used to describe the percentage of sales made at full price – the higher the sell through, the more popular the style and the less stock leftover. Naturally brands want to achieve as high a sell though as they can, but for those with a lot of stores achieving this is difficult because they have to put the whole size range in many of the stores. Even with a bestselling style, it's unrealistic to expect every store to sell all their stock, (this is why fringe sizes are only available in larger stores or online, it keeps the stock tight). If a brand has 100 stores and they send ten of each style to every store, even if eight sell, there are two left, across 100 stores that's 200 unsold dresses. Now imagine when a brand that has 500 stores, and 1000 styles! The amount of overstock soon adds up.

Generally, if a style has sold well and only a small percentage of stock remains there is no need to reduce heavily. The public liked it; they need little incentive to buy it for less. But if the left-over stock is concentrated on a couple of slow selling sizes, then the discount will have to be increased to shift those particular sizes – what a bonus when that size is yours! If a style sold poorly in all sizes, the discount is going to have to be pretty big to convince you to part with your cash.

As I said, there are so many reasons why something sells badly and it isn't always because of poor quality or awful design. Often it's timing and so some of the best bargains to be had are buying seasonal goods out of season. I'll happily admit to buying Christmas cards in January (the problem comes in October when I've forgotten that I bought them!).

Going back to my bargain wool coat for a moment, one of the reasons it was so cheap is because the logistical costs involved in storing and reselling it the following year are not commercially viable.

When a sale costs, rather than saves you money then you are not consuming sustainably (remember there are three pillars, environmental, social, and economic). You will end up with a wardrobe full of unwanted clothes, and a bank account somewhat emptier, not to mention the time that you will never get back. So, next time you head to the sale rail, think before you buy, are you comprising on style, colour and fit to save a few pounds? If so, is that money which would have been better saved up to purchase something that will return a better cost per wear? As the saying goes, "If something appears to be too good to be true, it usually is".

Just because it's not new, ***it doesn't mean it is old.***

13

Love, *Preloved*

When asked which clothes are the most sustainable? My answer is without doubt, the ones that already exist! Before you panic, I'm not suggesting we should never buy anything brand new again. I'm a realist and a pragmatist and I love buying new things but I want to share with you the reason why I love preloved.

Let's face it, preloved is just a trendy way of saying second hand, but don't make the mistake of thinking it refers only to musty old charity shops, selling clothes as old as your granny! These days the preloved space encompasses a whole range of options, from swapping to boutique style selling. If you are not already a convert, stay with me, this chapter will explore them all.

With the second-hand clothing market about to double to US$77 B in the next five years[1], there is little doubt that buying clothes 'new to you' is fashionable, and I could not be happier.

You've probably worn preloved in some form, at some point, in your life. As a child in the 1980's we wore preloved by necessity rather than choice. My mum's siblings would pass children's clothes between the cousins, ensuring no item went to waste. I loved receiving my cooler older cousins hand me downs. Unlike some people who went on to resent wearing cast offs, the thrill of receiving a bag filled with 'new to me' clothes, has not left me. I adore it when a friend passes me a potential new addition that they no longer want. I love that my friends and I have created a clothing merry-go-round for our children, and we enjoy looking at photos of the various children wearing our favourite pieces.

I've always instilled in my children that clothes are to be loved, worn, and then shared. They oversee their own wardrobe edits, often suggesting which of their younger friends may like a certain item next.

1 2021 Fashion Resale Market and Trend Report | thredUP

I am so encouraged by recent studies and reports that my passion for preloved is shared by the younger generation. In 2020 Mintel published a study, which revealed a changing opinion towards preloved in the UK, with more than half of the consumers in the key 25-34 age group buying second-hand fashion. This is a sentiment echoed in Hong Kong. A recent piece in China Daily reported that Millennials and Generation Z have become more aware of wasteful consumption and are now leading the charge in the second-hand market.

Despite this, there is a continued industry rhetoric of "buy new, buy often", driven by the need for brands to sell volume to be profitable. Over the years this has contributed to a view that clothes are disposable. Too many people buy and then discard clothes all too quickly. It's estimated that in the UK, the average lifetime for an item of clothing is 2.2[2] years and the picture is bleaker in Hong Kong. A recent study by NGO Redress revealed that two in five Hong Kongers only hold onto clothing for one year or less.

But let's get back to preloved. A recent edit of my own wardrobe showed that over two thirds of my

2 Clothing | WRAP

clothes were initially bought by someone else, so why do I shop this way, so often.

My motives are three-fold.

Honestly speaking, the first and perhaps most important reason I love preloved is that it enables me to purchase brands and designers, whose clothes I would seldom be able to afford if I purchased them new and at full price. In short, I can afford to buy better clothes!

Secondly, it allows me an opportunity to experiment with styles and colours without breaking the bank or feeling guilty that I might not love that particular look in the long term.

Lastly, I love that I breathe new life into unwanted or unworn clothes. Someone somewhere bought an item and then, for whatever reason, decided that it was no longer for them. Instead of it hanging unworn and unloved in their wardrobe (or worse, sent to landfill) it is now loved and worn by me!

So now you understand a little bit more about the why, let's go through the how. These days there are many different ways to consume preloved, at both ends of the scale, and while I could happily write a book dedicated solely to second-hand shopping, I will keep this to an overview of the most popular options.

Charity Shops

Let's start with charity shops as they are probably your biggest association with second-hand and they are genuinely one of my favourite places to shop. My love affair with charity shops started from a young age. My Nana and I would regularly pop in, and while my charity shop purchases were not always sartorial, it gave the shopaholic in me an excuse to buy!

I firmly believe that the thrill of curating an outfit for less or finding something unique to wear influenced the way I viewed second-hand clothing as I got older. The only time my love affair waned was during my later university years and into my early twenties. Unsurprisingly, this coincided with the height of Fast Fashion and the start of my career, working for one of the industry most famous Fast Fashion retailers. During this time, although, I frequented charity shops less, I did develop a passion for vintage. Sadly, this wasn't as affordable as my local Oxfam!

Family and friends aside, one of the things I miss most about living away from home is those afternoons spent pottering around the charity shops in my hometown, followed by a glass of wine with my school friends. It really is one of my favourite things to do and beats a visit to a fancy department store any day of the week.

British Author and TV personality Mary Portas in the 2009 BBC TV programme 'Mary Queen of Charity Shops', shone a light on the plight of UK charity shops. As someone who is passionate about keeping them relevant and prosperous, I was inspired by her overhaul of a local 'Save The Children' store. The show pioneered a new type of charity shopping and launched her premium charity retail proposition, Mary's Living & Giving. Ten years later there are now 25 shops across the UK which have raised over £30million for Save the Children. I was lucky enough to visit one and it goes without saying that I ended up a dress better off!

I'm a ***get a dress from the thrift shop*** *but* ***open a bottle of champagne*** *kind of person*

HELEN MIRREN

Re Sell Boutiques

These are becoming more popular, even here in Hong Kong. I first encountered the concept when I lived in London and some friends moved to suburbia. One of the things I love about visiting a new town is checking out the local shops. In areas that are not big enough to support the chains, there tends to be a High Street filled with independents. As well as the usual butchers, bakers, and green grocers there is often one of those card and gift shops which I describe to my husband as "the cute shop that sells all the nice things" and if I am really lucky, there's also an boutique or two.

While wandering down this particular High Street, I came across a clothes shop called 'The Frock Exchange' (A clever name, given its proximity to the 'City'). On closer inspection I realised it was a second-hand shop, but not one selling clothes for charity, as I was used to, but a fancier boutique style, that existed for profit. This concept is an outlet for women who want to claw back cash from items they no longer wear. The revenue is split between the individual seller and the shop owner, who shoulders the overheads but is not laden with the cash flow outlay and risk that comes with buying stock.

While living in London, I bought and sold countless outfits from there, and upon arriving in Hong Kong I tried, without luck, to seek out the same concept. It took time for preloved to catch on in Hong Kong but it's now thriving, both online and traditional retail. The clothes sold don't have to be designer, though increasingly they are. In part this is down to the fact that more and more High Street clothes are not made well enough to be passed on to multiple owners. The craftsmanship and superior fabrics used to create more expensive clothes often mean that they last longer and can be worn by more people. While many of us can only dream of buying designer clothes straight off the catwalk, acquiring beautiful pieces, a few seasons later, when the fashionistas are on to the next thing, has never been so accessible.

Online Marketplace

The explosion of eBay in the late 1990's enabled us to sell our unwanted clothes directly to others without having to set up a website or pay commission to a reseller. For many this was a game changer.

Selling in this way has pros and cons, but for me, as a consumer, the ability to track down a specific item without leaving my sofa was revolutionary. The emergence of premium denim brands, usually American, happened around the same time. If I wanted to get my hands on a particular pair of jeans, not only could I search the brand, but also the size, style, and wash, and the chances were high that someone somewhere wanted to sell second-hand, the exact pair I coveted.

Of course, this isn't risk free. We are at the mercy of the seller to ensure a true representation of the item is shown and for them to actually send it to us. As a seller I have had some bad luck when goods have 'not arrived'. A level of trust is definitely required and through reviews and feedback, both sellers and buyers have been able to build up a positive reputation.

Since the advent of eBay there have been many iterations and the explosion of social media has meant that it has been easier to connect with thousands of like-minded people all over the world. Singapore based classified marketplace, Carousell, has really taken off in Hong Kong. Since its launch in 2016, the online platform has served one in ten of the population.

Facebook groups for buying and selling all genres of clothes have become increasingly popular but are less regulated so trading with strangers comes with more risk.

Samples Sales

As child my Nana and my Aunt Lu would often take me to a jumble sale at a local church hall or community centre. These one-off sales in which miscellaneous second-hand items are sold to raise money for a cause, seem to be less common. But back in the day, I would love rooting about in the piles of clothes, in the hope there would be a hidden gem from my favourite shops such as Tammy Girl or Chelsea Girl.

Years later when as an Assistant Buyer, I went to my very first sample sale, it immediately took me right back to those 1980s jumbles!

For most of us working in fashion, the sample sale is the single biggest perk of the job. Piles upon piles of clothes, in varying conditions stacked high, costing next to (and sometimes) nothing. Any fashionistas dream! Some samples are the first iteration of a new design, others one of the many fitting samples a factory has to make before it can go into production. Often, a sale will include samples returned from photo shoots which are almost always in perfect condition. Occasionally there are even new garments, bought from another brand and used for 'inspiration' or as part of a competitor shopping report. In the height of

Marc Jacobs mania, I managed to find at the bottom of a box, a brand-new, complete with tags blazer, by the man himself, I bought it with change of a fiver!

While the sales can be incredible, most of the time the garments are the factories mistakes and design interpretations gone wrong. The waste is shocking. Years ago, it didn't matter to me that part of the garment was ripped, or missing a button or wrongly sized, these were (almost free) clothes and when I was 23 and styling myself in one of the world's most expensive cities, I learnt to make do and mend. I was hooked on the concept of taking unwanted clothes and making them work for me.

These days samples sales are held both internally for employees only and also more formally arranged events for friends, family, and VIPs. The items on sale vary in terms of their condition, from early development that might fit like a sack of potatoes, or be in a suspect fabric, to garments that have nothing 'wrong' with them except perhaps the Buyer wanted to change the colour or the buttons or a pocket or whatever. If you get lucky there may even be some salesman's samples, these are perfect pre-production examples that are used to sell the range to potential buyers.

Samples sell for a fraction of the retail price as brands or factories try to recoup some of the overhead that this complex and time-consuming process creates. Depending on the brand, up to 15 to 20 samples can be made before a garment is given the green light to go into full production. When you are making tens of thousands, you can ill afford any mistakes or misinterpretations. With advances in 3D technology and with new ways of selling imposed by the pandemic, there is more evidence to suggest that many of these samples are not needed.

In Hong Kong, there are shops dedicated to selling samples and slight seconds which have been produced in factories over the border. You can find some gems here if you are willing to pop in frequently and be patient.

Dead Stock Sales

Incinerating unwanted yet useable clothing, known as dead stock, is not a new phenomenon for retailers. It recently captured the public's attention when an exposé of high-end designer brands literally burning clothes costing more than most people's monthly salary, went public. This is justified because the overproduction creates fear that excessive mark downs and stock entering the marketplace will cause a devaluation of the brand.

Campaigners globally are calling for a ban on this practice. Orsola de Castro, co-founder and global creative director at sustainability campaign group Fashion Revolution, said "*Nobody ought to be surprised that retailers are burning excess stock, but despite it being one of the fashion industry's most open secrets, it is finally being seen for what it is: madness.*".

In France, under the anti-waste law, it's now illegal to destroy leftover stock. In the UK a parliamentary committee report on sustainability and the fashion industry published in 2019 considered the various environmental impacts of incineration. The report advised the government to ban the burning or dumping of unsold stock if it can be reused or recycled. Those calls were rejected.

Brands are more than aware that this practice is bad PR and have been looking for alternative ways to clear their overstock. One solution has been the emergence of independent third-party businesses selling differing brands 'dead stock'. This concept is different to the outlet village model, where a brand has its own shop dedicated to past seasons styles that they have been unable to sell, these out-of-town retail 'villages' are home to a large number of retailers, and customers often come from afar for day out and to grab a bargain, designer or otherwise. As a side note on that concept, many of the clothes on sale there, were made especially for these outlets, and are not always the premium stock that customers think they are buying. Third-party dead stock sales are kind of like a last chance saloon for unsold clothes. While there is no arguing that this is great way to get a bargain, the concept exists only because of global over production. Nearly 20% of garments made go unsold and The Boston Consulting Group predicts that if we do not change our habits, global fashion sales will increase from 62 million tons to 102 million tons by 2030[3] This huge excess, is one of fashions biggest problems that needs to be reversed.

My own feeling towards this type of shopping is mixed, these clothes have been made, we can't get back the resources used to make them, and if they're not sold it's likely they'll be destroyed. This benefits no one and is waste of the worst possible kind.

I have reaped the rewards of this kind of sale. A few years ago, while walking through an upscale mall I spotted a dress in the window of an international

3 The High Price of Fast Fashion - WSJ

brand. It stopped me in my tracks, I loved it, the shape and the colour were perfect. I couldn't justify the price tag, so in accordance with my pre purchase check list, (see chapter one) I walked away. Around a year later, I was at a dead stock sale that featured said brand, I walked in and there was my dress, in the same colour and in my size. I bought it at only 25% of the original price and have worn it so many times. It started life as my Christmas Day dress and has since been restyled to enjoy outings to the office, as well as to dinners and conferences. So, from that perspective, I saved that dress from the incinerator, but in doing so I have to ask myself if I am part of the problem, encouraging brands to over produce knowing there will always be an outlet?

I don't pretend to have all the answers, this is a complex issue and sometimes we just need to do what we think is best at that time, depending on our circumstance. Changing our view as we become more informed is okay. There is nothing more frustrating than the notion that when we hold a certain view, we must be married to it forever more.

Swapping

This is without doubt one of the most fun things fashion lovers can do. Swap parties are a great way to update your wardrobe without spending any money. The concept is simple, you exchange pieces that you no longer love, nor wear for items that you will. The swap can be amongst a few friends for fun or it can be arranged on a bigger scale, within communities to raise funds for good causes. It can be as big or as small as you want. I am so passionate about swap parties, that since 2011, I have hosted a charity 'Frock Swap' at least once a year.

Back when I first arrived in Hong Kong, I quickly became frustrated with the lack of shops that catered to me. At that time, only a handful of the predictable global brands operated here. Ecommerce still hadn't taken off with any authority and so often when I turned up at a social event, there would be at least a couple of other women in the same outfit! So many of us were getting tired of the clothes we had, and so the idea was born.

This chapter is in no way meant to persuade you to never buy anything new again, far from it. I love buying brand new clothes and I have no intention of stopping.

Why Swap?

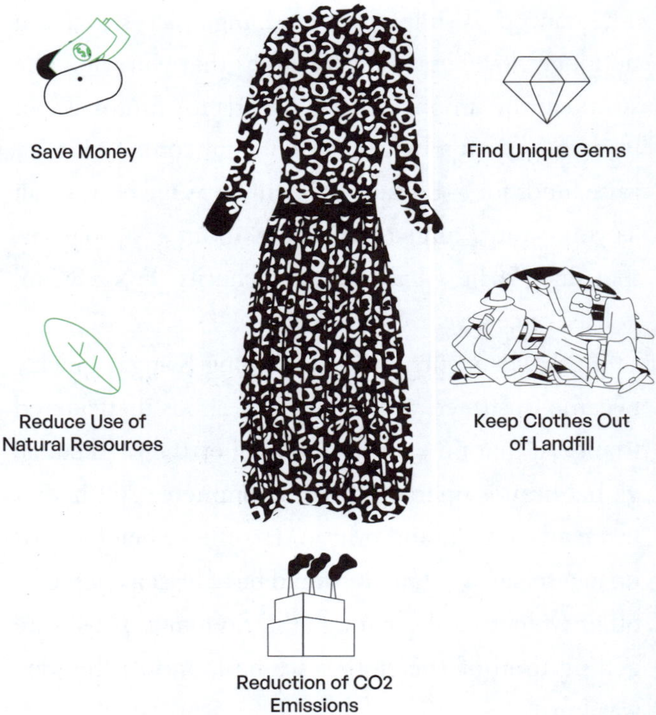
Save Money
Find Unique Gems
Reduce Use of Natural Resources
Keep Clothes Out of Landfill
Reduction of CO2 Emissions

It's just that I buy less brand new, and when I do, I ensure it is something that I really want and will wear for years to come. I very much subscribe to the notion that 'every little helps', so when I read the statistic by the ethical business community #Ethical Hour, that

If one million women bought their next item of clothing second hand instead of new, we would save 6 million kgs of carbon pollution from entering the atmosphere,

It really resonated. In a time where the impact of climate change is real, buying some of our clothes second hand is an easy change that we can all make to reduce our impact and in doing so we can save ourselves money too!

Well-made and cared for clothes will last a lifetime, sometimes two, so let's enable that. I hope that next time you fancy a new addition you'll take a look at your 'new to you' options. In ending this ode to preloved, I urge you to organise a frock swap of your own, I promise it will be a fabulous night.

There is ***no beauty in the finest cloth if it makes hunger and unhappiness***

MAHATNA GANDHI

14
Fabric *Matters*

Aside from keeping your unwanted clothes out of landfill, choosing which fabric your clothes are made from is probably the next biggest decision you can make, in having a direct and positive impact on how sustainable your wardrobe really is. There are countless blogs, books and studies written about the environmental and social impact of the different fibres and fabrics used to construct our clothes. You could easily spend days reading up on the topic. But I want to keep this as simple as the complexities and nuances allow.

I'll start by saying there is no perfect answer.

No one magic fibre can be produced at scale that avoids any negative impact. Every option has its pros and cons, some more than others of course. The fabrics you chose to buy and wear will be guided by what you think is important.

In summary, there are two main types of materials: natural and synthetic. Those that occur in nature, like cotton and those that are man-made, such as polyester. These two categories can be further broken down, but to avoid getting over complicated, I have grouped the types of clothing materials into four categories, Synthetic, Semi Synthetic Plant, and Animal. We'll look at each group.

Synthetics

Fabrics made from virgin synthetic fibres are the least sustainable and should, where possible, be avoided or limited, when curating your guilt-free wardrobe. These synthetic fibres are derived from petroleum and made of a complex molecular structure. The method in which they are produced is highly energy intensive. Not surprisingly they are non-biodegradable and sadly, due to their low cost, are some of the most common fibres used in clothing production. Shockingly in 2018, polyester made up 52% of global fibre production[1].

The problem with synthetic fabrics doesn't just stop at production. Every time you wash a synthetic garment, microfibres are released into the water and ultimately end up in our rivers, oceans, and food chain.

A study by Plymouth University found that acrylic was the worst offender, releasing nearly 730,000 tiny synthetic particles per wash. This is 1.5 times as many as polyester. The full extent of the impact of these microplastics is not yet known, but the problem is significant.

1 Analyst Briefing ITMA Barcelona (oerlikon.com)

Every fibre or material has its advantages and synthetics are no exception. Garments made from fabrics using these fibres really do last a long time. They require less water, energy, and heat for washing. A 30-degree wash works every time! Typically, they are inexpensive and hardwearing, which explains why clothes made of these fabrics are so prevalent. But it's not just about cost.

These fabrics are wildly versatile and so are massively attractive to many different types of clothing producers. They can be used as a performance textile in sports and outdoor wear and there is no denying that technological advances in this sector have created some premium and good-looking fabrics, particularly those replicating silk, fur, and suede. For some consumers, they offer an attractive vegan alternative, but generally the motive is cost.

There is no getting away from polyester's association with fast and cheap fashion, which, let's be honest, can look naff, especially in black, where it is often shiny and shoddy looking.

Your sustainable wardrobe should be filled with clothes that can be worn for many years, to make this possible choosing the right fabric for the right garment is critical. Realistically, there is no point using a more sustainable option if the fabric isn't fit for purpose. It won't last and all the resource used to create it will have been in waste. It is important to accept that a substitute won't always deliver the same fit, attributes or practicalities for say swimwear or active wear for example. But this is where the 'eco' versions of synthetic fabric come into their own.

The number of companies producing garments made from more sustainable iterations of these synthetic fabrics such as recycled polyester and Econyl, is growing.

In many cases the materials being recycled are post-consumer plastic and in particular plastic bottles. These single use drinks bottles are usually made from polyethylene terephthalate (PET) which thankfully, can be recycled or perhaps more accurately described as 'downcycled', given whatever it becomes will inevitably be of lower quality than the original product. The heating process shortens polymer chains, thus degrading the plastic quality.

On the surface, this is positive. None of us want to see these discarded plastic bottles clogging up our streets, beaches, and oceans. It's sickening.

But for me, recycling is the best worst option. Mass recycling, of anything, usually consumes high levels of energy, can be expensive and still requires a mix of virgin materials to create something new.

Of course, it is preferable to utilise this waste than send it to landfill. Additionally the recycled iteration of these synthetics has a reduced impact, compared to their virgin equivalent, but it does pose the question, by making plastic bottles a saleable commodity, are we justifying or even encouraging their use?

Perhaps it would be wiser to reduce the amount of single use plastics and develop alternate, more sustainable options.

Plant Based

Natural fabrics get a lot of good 'green' press, the perception is that they derive from nature and will biodegrade at the end of their life cycle. Because of this, they are often considered to be more sustainable than their synthetic counterparts which can take decades if not hundreds of years to decompose. But as I said right back at the beginning, sustainability is about much more than just the environmental impact. We need to consider social and economic impact too.

There are many natural fabrics that are commonly used for making clothes, the two most well-known being cotton and linen.

Linen, made from the fibres of the flax plant, is durable, absorbs water and has an ability to keep people cool and is deemed as very sustainable. Not often viewed as 'fashionable' (personally I think it can be chic and timelessly stylish) and perhaps seen as a bit of a one hit wonder in a 'holiday' fabric kind of a way.

Almost three-quarters of flax is grown in the EU, where geographical conditions mean, it is produced using less water than cotton and requires no pesticides and is good for soil health. The additional bonus is that it is naturally moth resistant and has natural colours such as ivory and ecru, meaning it can be used without additional dying.

So why aren't we using it more?

In a nutshell, cost. Harvesting flax is laborious, with the time from seed to harvest around 90 days. The overheads and expenses of producing in Western European countries is high, and so the cost of growing flax is more than that of growing cotton. Flax fibres are fragile and can break easily. Weaving linen into a usable fabric, at scale, also requires machinery that runs slower. So basically, a lot less linen is produced in the comparable timeframe to cotton.

There have been scores written on the benefits and hazards of cotton production so I will keep my perspective brief.

Like most natural fabrics, cotton biodegrades well but when it's mixed with other (usually synthetic) fibres it becomes more challenging. Cotton can be grown naturally, but mass farming usually requires the intensive use of pesticides and chemicals, as well as gallons of water. Its production is also labour and resource intensive.

Thankfully, increasingly sustainable ways of producing the fabric are becoming widespread. The Better Cotton Initiative (BCI), whose mission is to "help cotton communities survive and thrive while protecting and restoring the environment", celebrated its 10th anniversary in 2019, and now accounts for 22% of global cotton production[2]. The organisation supports cotton farmers across the world, helping them to care for the water, soil health and natural habitats used in cotton production with certain specifications. Many brands have made BCI cotton standard or are working towards a full adoption.

Organic and Fairtrade cottons are widely recognised as being more sustainable. Clothes made using either of these types of cotton carry a distinctive hangtag to highlight their certification to a customer.

The Global Organic Textile Standard (GOTS) is an internationally recognised organic textile standard founded in 2006. This certification guarantees that the cotton in the product you are buying, was produced without use of toxic fertilisers or pesticides which are harmful to the environment and those who work with it.

Fairtrade accredited cotton encourages sustainable cotton production and is the only standard to provide economic benefits, through a guaranteed 'Fairtrade

2 Sustainable Cotton Reaches 22% of Global Production as 2.3 Million Farmers Receive Training on Improved Agricultural Practices - Better Cotton

Minimum Price' and additional 'Fairtrade Premium' for seed cotton farmers. A study on the impact of the use of Fairtrade cotton in four countries particularly noted the positive impact of Fairtrade standards on gender equity[3]. Studies show that women's role in farming has increased over time, and traditionally they have had less access to land, information, credit, and training and as in many sectors, historically overlooked for leadership roles[4]. Fairtrade helps to address this imbalance by supporting and empowering women to participate equally in agriculture[5]. This is a positive step forward and by buying clothes with the Fairtrade tag you can help support this.

The contemporary problems and challenges associated with cotton have arisen in part because demand has basically outstripped supply. What could be a very sustainable fibre has in some places become an ethical and political minefield that is creating further instability within the supply chain.

Chinese produced cotton has come under increased scrutiny and in 2020, The Better Cotton Initiative suspended its activities in Xinjiang due to its

3 About Cotton - Fairtrade Foundation

4 Gender strategy 2016-2020: Transforming equal opportunity, access and benefits for all - (fairtrade.net)

5 SDG5: Gender equality - (fairtrade.net)

concerns, resulting in a significant drop in the region's cotton exports. In June 2021, The Cotton China Sustainable Development Program was officially launched by the China Cotton Association (CCA), with the goal of creating a homegrown independent sustainable standard and certification system.

Animal Based

There are many, but let's focus on those we are the most familiar with - wool, silk, and leather.

Wool is considered to be a sustainable fibre. It's renewable, durable, and biodegradable. It has strength and resilience (being both flame-resistant and water-repellent) giving the clothes that are made from it a sense of longevity.

Some sheep farmers are now producing wool using techniques that sequester carbon from the atmosphere, further reducing its environmental impact[6]. Yet despite this, the use of wool in clothing is not free of its critics.

Undoubtedly not all wool farms have adequate welfare standards. Buying wool from a brand whose suppliers share your values is important when curating your guilt-free wardrobe. Look for garments made with wool that conforms to the Responsible Wool Standard, a voluntary standard that addresses the welfare of sheep and the land they graze on.

Categorising leather as sustainable is debatable and, at times, controversial. Many brands have already banned the use of exotic animal skins and fur, but for

6 This "Climate Beneficial" Wool Hat Comes From Carbon-Positive Sheep (fastcompany.com)

most, leather is still a commonly used material. As the skin of a dead creature, it will never be considered animal friendly. Usually, the hides are a by-product of animals raised for their meat. Some argue that by using the skin in the production of leather products it minimises waste. Hides are kept out of landfill and, as these animals are being reared regardless, leather does not require additional land and resource.

Others argue that practises in the meat industry are questionable at best and totally unethical at worse. But this isn't a book on veganism.

To be usable, the hides must be tanned, a process of soaking the animal skin in a liquid tannic acid, or by the use of other chemicals. One of the most popular ways to do this is through a process called chrome tanning. This involves the use of chemicals which if not handled correctly can allow toxic effluents to become present in the watershed[7] causing dermal and respiratory damage to tannery workers and can have infiltrate the local drinking water supply[8].

The alternative is a vegetable tanning process, but seldom used at scale due to the cost and skills involved. Vegetable-tanned leather is considered higher quality

7 Leather tanning (productip.com)
8 Chromium Contamination in Tannery Effluent (pharosproject.net)

and will last longer than synthetically treated leather. It takes longer to make, which is part of the reason why vegetable-tanned leather only makes up roughly 10% of all leather available today[9].

Leather is durable and long lasting, often looking more stylish when battered and worn. So, when curating your sustainable wardrobe, it's always a good idea to consider second-hand leather, charity shops often carry tremendous finds in this category. I could not hide my delight when last year I picked up a vintage Italian leather jacket for the equivalent of only HK$100 in the Cathedral preloved shop!

9 Why Vegetable Tanned Leather Is so Expensive and Rare (businessinsider.com)

SEMI SYNTHETICS

Finally, there are a whole group of mostly cellulose fibres, that are classed as semi synthetic and carry a lower environment impact. Cellulose is a natural polymer derived from wood and other agricultural pulp. Examples include Rayon, Viscose, Lyocell, and new innovative fabrics such as pineapple fibre!

Most of these cellulosic fabrics start their journey as trees. Forrest conversation charity, Canopy has found that ancient and endangered forests are increasingly making their way into clothing. Every year, 3.2 billion trees are cut down to make paper packaging or fabrics such as rayon and viscose[10]. Nicole Rycroft, Executive Director of Canopy says, "Systemic change in fibre sourcing is becoming unavoidable." The charity has partnered with over 25 retailers and designers, including High Street regulars Zara, H&M, and Marks and Spencer, as well as sustainable luxury pioneers, Eileen Fisher, Patagonia, and Stella McCartney, all of whom have committed to eliminate their use of fabrics that contain endangered forest fibre.

10 Deforestation: So out of style - Canopy (canopyplanet.org)

Lyocell, produced under the trade name Tencel, like viscose, is made from a cellulose. It is a popular choice of fabric for many sustainable brands. It is versatile and depending on the fibre length chosen, it can result in fabric of different thicknesses and textures. It is used in a whole range of clothing, including dresses, underwear, and activewear. It is pure white when produced, so no bleaching is necessary.

The fabric (as long as it is not mixed with synthetic fibres) biodegrades quicker than fully synthetic alternatives and it is compostable. The production of Tencel has a lower environmental footprint compared with viscose and rayon and Lenzing AG, parent owner of the brand, states it only sources from sustainably managed PEFC or FSC tree plantations. The process used in its chemical treatment phase ensures almost no solvent is dumped into the ecosystem. Naturally, it is more expensive than its non-branded equivalents.

Piñatex is a leather substitute made from the leaves of pineapples grown in the Philippines. Its production is much more sustainable than traditional leather because it is completely animal-free, requires less water and no harmful chemicals are used in its production. The leftover leaf waste is recycled and used for fertiliser or biomass, so it really is a bit of an all-rounder! Along with other fruit and animal 'leathers' I think this an area to watch.

The reality is, many of our clothes are made from complex combinations of fibres, a problematic blend of natural yarns, man-made filaments, plastics, and metals, making them difficult to break down. Our beloved jeans are a great example here.

Usually made from cotton yarn, 'denim' tends to be blended with a synthetic element like elastane, to give us an enhanced fit. Jeans also contain many other components such as zips, buttons and polyester sewing threads and that is before we account for chemicals used in the dyeing and finishing process.

While we are talking about denim, I think it is worth noting that of all fabrics, this is perhaps the one that has gone through the biggest sustainable revolution. According to a piece by Kayley Roshitsh of Women's Wear Daily, "Denim scrutiny has led the sector to "innovate faster," with hope to inspire the rest of the fashion industry in its sustainability journey"

Conventional methods use high quantities of water and chemicals in the washing, dyeing, and finishing process, while production is labour intensive. The wastewater can often be polluting to the local environment and the toxins in the dyeing and finishing process harmful to workers.

The sector as a whole has been stepping up its efforts in terms of ecological innovations and has been making progress in the last decade. Some manufacturers have opted to switch to new technologies, introduce more efficient manufacturing processes and employ techniques that reduce water consumption. As a result, we are seeing contemporary denim being produced in a far more responsible way, using less water, energy, and fewer chemicals.

The adoption of laser technology by many brands as an alternate way to achieve denim finishes like sandblasting and stone washing, has reduced environmental impact as it eliminates the need for water, stones, or sand to create the desired effects.

Traditionally, bleach is used to fade denim but the development of ozone technology, which harnesses the natural bleaching capabilities of ozone gas to give a range of bleach effects, has substantially reduced negative environmental impact. Unlike lasering, ozone does not eliminate water use but it does substantially reduce its consumption as well that of energy, chemicals, enzymes, and stones.

In 2019, Dutch denim brand, Denham introduced the first biodegradable stretch denim. Using organic cotton wrapped around a natural rubber core, it's free from plastics and microplastics.

As demand for sustainable alternatives grow, more money is being invested in the research and development of exciting innovations, not only in fibre production, but fibre recycling too. These could be potential game changers if they can be scaled and produced in enough mass to make a difference.

Sequins are an area where innovation is needed. We all love a bit of sparkle now and again, but traditional sequins are a sustainability nightmare. They are made from petroleum plastics and synthetic resin. They cannot biodegrade and are unfortunately prevalent in inexpensive fashion that tends to end up in landfill not long after it is purchased.

In 2019 Oxfam reported that 1.7 million sequined items would end up in landfill after the Christmas period, despite having been worn a measly average of five times. I love a sequin! But I buy them sparingly and only on items I know I will cherish for years to come.

However, there is a light on the horizon as The Sustainable Sequin Company, based in London, have received funding to continue their research in developing biodegradable sequins.

Innovations like this are exciting but need support from consumers. Keep an eye out for when brands launch these types of innovations and support them. Like with all business, it's the supply and demand that keeps them going.

It's not just the materials used to make our clothes that we should consider. The finished garments need to be shipped around the world, usually by sea, from producer to consumer in a way that limits damage. Plastic bags are usually the packaging of choice because they are inexpensive, they keep the item clean, dry, and in the best condition for sale. With billions of items being produced each year, the scale of accompanying plastic bags is frightening. The number of bags made from recycled materials, or that are able to be recycled, has grown but the fact remains, these are ultimately single use.

Again, advances in technology and innovation have led to alternatives. While working for an independent brand I was introduced to a company that had created a sustainable solution - a bag that looked and functioned like plastic but was made from Hydroplast film. The bag is 100% water soluble, biodegradable, compostable, and marine safe. When placed in hot water it totally disappears. This blew my mind! When I asked why it wasn't being implemented by every retailer under the sun, the answer was unsurprisingly related to cost. I was told the increase was only cents more than a conventional bag, an insignificant amount to the shopper, when compared to the retail price. But for many retailers who are producing millions of items a year, those cents add up and very few are actually willing to invest, or sacrifice, that kind of money to make a real difference. So next time your online delivery arrives - check out the type of bag it came in and ask questions if you want to see change.

The main takeaway from this chapter is that fabric sustainability is multi-faceted and complex!

My advice is thus, where you can, opt for a more responsibly sourced or more sustainably produced alternative and avoid virgin materials. By shopping second hand and wearing your clothes for longer, you are helping to reduce the demand for new fabric. It's that simple. You can make a difference.

No one wants your cheap, old clothes, *not even the neediest people on earth.*

JARED T. MILLER

15

End of *Life*

There comes a time in the lives of all clothes, when there is no amount of restyling, mending, and reworking that can save that beloved piece. It can be hard to let go of a favourite, an item that has been with you through the good times and bad, fat days and thin. Perhaps it's a sentimental piece, or just something that felt very comfortable to wear. Either way, you know deep down that it's past its best and can't be passed on.

The good news is that there are alternatives that don't involve 'throwing it away'; a commonly used phrase and something that many of us do, without actually stopping to think about where 'away' is.

> *There is* ***no such thing as away****.*
> *When you throw something away,*
> ***it must go somewhere****.*

When we talk about clothing, especially items that have reached the end of their life, 'away' often equals landfill. We all know now, that sending clothes to landfill just isn't the answer.

People ask why so much textile waste ends up in landfill. It's all too easy to blame it on laziness and a lack of effort, but I don't believe that's always the case. The reasons are plenty.

Firstly, there is so much clothing waste. Globally we have an over consumption problem that is simply not being addressed. The reasons for which are complex, but in short, I believe it's driven by an insatiable need to buy more, from an industry who understandably doesn't want to reduce the amount it produces. Realistically, what business would?

I also think there's a lack of education on the subject, especially for people of my generation. I learned a lot of academic content at school that I haven't had use for since, and conversely, there were so many practical aspects that were simply not explained – understanding the impact of waste on the environment was one of them. Perhaps environmental matters just weren't so prevalent then as they are now. Ironically this is why we are in this mess!

However, I am massively encouraged to learn that this is changing. My own children are far more knowledgeable on the subject than I ever was at their age.

The lack of education is also compounded by a lack of alternatives to the household bin. Access to textile recycling banks is very much dependent on the resources available in an area. Hong Kong's Home Affairs Department launched a "Community Used Clothes Recycling Bank Scheme" in 2006, to allow the public to donate used clothes in support of environmental protection. The scheme is a partnership between Government, District Councils and NGOs. Currently it is run by Friends of the Earth (Hong Kong), Christian Action, Salvation Army and Conservancy Association.

In the U.S, 85% of unwanted clothing is either burnt or sent to landfill[1] and a recent EU study based on 15 member countries and the UK, indicated that only 10% of all textile waste remains in use through the second-hand market.[2] In disposing of unwanted clothes, we're left with unconscionable waste.

---

1 Textiles: Material-Specific Data | US EPA
2 Fashion waste index – LABFRESH

According to a report by European Commission's Institute for Prospective Technological Studies (IPTS) a mere 8% of discarded clothes are returned to the production cycle via recycling, the remaining are permanently disposed of. A shocking 24.3% are incinerated in a CO2 intensive process. And a frightening 57.1%, (yes, more than half) of unwanted clothes end up in landfill[3].

Breaking down old clothes into fibres to make new clothes, is a challenge so many are looking to solve. The difficulties lie in the complex mix of fibres that most clothes are comprised of, not to mention all the trims used too. American designer Eileen Fisher has been working in this area and through her take back programme has had thousands of unwanted garments returned to be repurposed, resold, or recycled. Speaking on a 2021 Business of Fashion podcast, she admitted how difficult the process has been, manpower and space as well as lack of technology makes the progression slow.

Hong Kong textiles company, Novotex is looking to solve this problem. It has developed a new and innovative technology that enables brands to revive

---

3 Microsoft Word - 120423 IMPRO Textiles_Publication draft v1.doc (europa.eu)

excess inventory, unused raw materials, or textile waste. Named, The Billie System, this mechanical recycling system does not consume water or produce chemical waste, unlike traditional recycling processes which require high volumes of both, to make useable yarns. The patented system is almost entirely automated, thereby reducing the high labour costs associated with textile recycling. It will be interesting to see how quickly this is scaled and adapted within the industry.

What I find so infuriating is that too many of the 57% of those clothes in landfill were disposed of prematurely and unnecessarily. I've lost count of the number of times I've opened a bin in my apartment block, only to find perfectly good clothes just sitting inside.

Take inspiration from these suggestions for ways you can repurpose basic items to ensure your clothes don't meet an inappropriate end.

- Cut old T-shirts and jersey items into rags and use them for cleaning, this saves having to buy cleaning cloths too!
- For slogan, embroidered or sentimental pieces, cut them into squares to make a memory blanket or cushion. My children have a huge cushion made from their baby clothes and it makes me smile every day. A quilt version is popular with teens who want to have their sports or school items made into a blanket or a throw, what a great way to keep these sentimental items in play for longer.
- During Covid lockdown my daughter took an interest in sewing, we were making hair scrunchies. For the inner elastic, we repurposed old knicker elastic. "Waste not want not", as they say.
- Remove the buttons and trims from items and use them for crafts – the added advantage is by removing the hardware you make it easier for the garment to be recycled.

- Get creative. Cut up the fabric to make doll's clothes, cover notebooks or use as patches on denim – the possibilities are endless.
- Natural fibres can be cut up for composting (no trims allowed!)

For those clothes that have not yet reached the end of their life, but are no longer wanted, of course dropping off at a recycling bank is better than putting in a generic bin, but often the clothes discarded at these collection banks are not recycled or donated effectively so use these as a last resort.

It should go without saying, (but I'll say it anyway), if the piece has been loved, worn and is still in good condition, then give someone else the opportunity to love and wear it!

If recouping money from a previous purchase is not of importance to you, then the quickest and easiest way to avoid it ending up in landfill, is to give it to a friend or donate it to a clothes swap.

If the item was hardly worn (and still relevant, or a timeless classic), or it still has the tags on (you are not alone here!), perhaps it's designer or from premium brand, then you could sell it through any of preloved channels discussed in chapter thirteen, Love Preloved. The beauty of preloved is that it is circular, enabling both buyer and seller to benefit, if you go on to reinvest the money earned by selling, back into the second-hand market, you truly do close the loop.

If all of that seems too much like hard work, the most popular option is to donate it to a charity shop. Donating clothes to charity is often used as a way for consumers to clear their conscience, passing on the responsibility of textile waste to others.

The reality is that most charities are over worked, underfunded, and drowning in poor-quality clothes, that no one wants to buy. As a result, many are shipped overseas to where the problem then belongs to someone else.

Charities have seen a real decline in the quality of their donations. At one of Oxfam's UK Wastesaver clothing sorting centres, 80 tonnes of cast-off clothing passes through each week. Most of these items will never be worn again.

The poor quality, and original low price of this kind of donation, make it unviable to sell. Let's face it, why would any charity waste their limited resources trying sell a second rate, second-hand top, that only cost a couple of pounds more to buy brand new?

Sorting through and separating bin bags full of stained, soiled, and unwearable clothes requires human resource. Which would be much better deployed hanging, steaming, and visual merchandising those preloved clothes that will sell. The process is labour intensive and usually done manually by volunteers. I know this, I've done it.

One of the things that really inspired me to significantly change my own consumption habits, was my experience volunteering for Redress. A Hong Kong based NGO campaigning to eliminate textile waste to landfill and improve circularity and sustainability within the fashion industry. During every campaign I worked on, I was left speechless at the scale and difference in donations, everything from saggy under garments to immaculate designer dresses had been left in recycling bins all over the city. It was mind boggling!

The reality is that most donations don't make the shop floor, and even those that do, don't sell in the volume that can make enough of a positive impact. But what happens to those clothes that can't be sold?

In Oxfam's case, 35% of the clothes go to their partners in Senegal to be sold, but the majority is sent to be recycled in some way. Those that are not able to be recycled, are simply torn up so they can be used as industrial cleaning cloths and stuffing for mattresses or car seats.

Oxfam are not alone; many charities send their donations to third world countries. This is complex and at times political.

Where these donations end up varies. Unwanted textile waste is shipped globally, according to data from Statista, in 2020 the UK exported over 232 million U.S dollars' worth of used clothing, Ghana was the top destination with approximately 72.4 million U.S dollars' worth. The reality is that your old clothes often end up as a tradable commodity, a saleable asset. But for whose benefit?

An extensive study conducted by the Institute of Economic Affairs in Kenya[4], in April 2021, on the used clothing industry found that it directly employs around two million people. The majority, 91.5%, of households in Kenya are said to purchase second-hand clothes. Which results in a significant reduction in greenhouse gas emissions and the use of toxins that would have been caused by the production of new textiles.[5]

4 The State of Second-Hand Clothes and Footwear Trade in Kenya IEA Kenya

5 BIR - BIR in the press - Global used clothing industry team up to 'dispel myths' about textile recycling

Research by Dr Andrew Brooks, Senior Lecturer in Development and Environment at Kings College London, found that white dress-shirts are regularly bound for Pakistan, where there is a great demand for them among lawyers. Warm coats most often travel to Eastern Europe, and short-sleeved tops and shorts, perhaps predictably, end up in Africa[6]. This can be seen as positive.

But there is also a negative impact. Dr Brooks argues that the flow of old clothing from the Western world, as well as the availability of cheap, new garments from East Asia, has had a negative effect on local textile industries in many countries. It truly is a global crisis.

The Covid-19 pandemic has negatively affected the second-hand supply chain. As people have been stuck at home they have decluttered on mass, clothing banks have been deluged with donations and as a result storage and sorting facilities have run out of room. Exporters have faced challenges moving the stock due to temporary import bans, (fearing clothes could carry the virus) and simultaneously the cost of logistics has risen dramatically. Antonio de Carvalho, of Green World Recycling, in central England, told Reuters that

6 Andrew Brooks (clothingpoverty.com)

the price he has been able to charge overseas buyers had dropped from £570 pounds a tonne to £400 pounds, making it hard for his company to cover the costs of collecting and storing items, to the point it was no longer commercially viable to send these unwanted items overseas. Without this supply chain it becomes even harder to keep unwanted clothing out of landfill.

Australian journalist, Linton Besser's eye-opening documentary, Dead White Man's Clothes, made in Ghana for ABC Australia reveals the clothing mountains, created over decades as a result of western retailers dumping their overstock, is well worth a watch on You Tube. For similar viewing I also recommend True Cost, Andrew Morgan's 2017 documentary which tells the story of the human and environmental impact of fashion, and more recently Joanna's Bowers 2021 documentary, Refashioned, which follows the journey of three Hong Kong changemakers who are creating solutions to the negative impacts of fashion.

Solving this clothing crisis is not simple but buying less and buying better will begin to eliminate the problem, as over time, it naturally reduces the amount of clothing in circulation. When we do let go of pieces, we have to be mindful of what and how we donate. We should remember that for charities to make money for their cause, they must receive quality donations, items that people like you and I want to buy. Please donate responsibly. Ensure your items are in clean and in good condition. Keep matching items together, fold them and put them in a closed bag to keep them that way.

Something to ponder here is, don't donate it if you wouldn't buy it.

Fashion likes nothing less than ***not being fashionable***

GAIL GALLIE

16

What's the *Alternative?*

In a utopian universe, all our clothes would be produced using natural, renewable or regenerative resources, sewn or assembled by skilled workers and craftsmen who get paid at least a living wage. The carbon emissions of transport, logistics and retail would be off set.

Sadly, this is not our reality, yet.

The fashion industry is far from immune to criticism when it comes to climate change. The industry has a lot of catching up to do when compared to the advances other sectors such as, food, ocean, and automobile have made in transforming their sustainable practices.

But the fashion industry hates being behind the curve of any trend, and sustainability is no exception. The size, complexity, and global nature of the sector makes it difficult to coordinate change.

The idea of 'Slow Fashion' is growing in popularity and brands advocating this are becoming more visible. But what is Slow Fashion?

Slow Fashion is an approach to clothing production which takes into consideration all aspects of the supply chain, aims to respect people, the environment, and animals.[1] There is a belief that clothes should be produced in a way that is more sustainable, it advocates fair wages for workers and places an emphasis on promoting artisanal skill and using natural fibres or sustainable technologies. Slow fashion supports the idea that clothes should be loved, a belief that it is quality over quantity and that clothes should be bought to last and enjoyed for many years. Seems like a good idea to me!

The 'problem' with 'Slow Fashion' as a solution is that its principles are not compatible with mass production on the scale that meets the demands of a growing global population. The global apparel market is projected to grow in value from US$1.5 trillion in 2020 to about US$2.25 trillion by 2025[2]. By its very nature, slow fashion takes longer and is more expensive. This is a price many cannot or will not pay.

---

1 What Does Slow Fashion 'Actually' Mean? (forbes.com)
2 Global Apparel Market - Statistics & Facts | Statista

Price aside, there are other barriers that stop us buying from brands who put ethics front and centre. As someone who has worked in the industry for two decades, I know that sustainable fashion is much more than its tired old stereotype: overpriced, beige linen and hippy tie dye. The challenge is to convince everyone else of the same.

There are brands whose purpose is to be sustainable, it is in their DNA and informs all their decisions, from designing with circulatory in mind to limiting their use of natural resources to how they manage the end-of-life process. It is important for those brands who have sustainability at their core to be financially sustainable. To achieve this, they must compete with regular fashion retailers, many of whom have more marketing spend and lower prices. It is not good enough just to register with customers. Their products must be appealing enough to convert them. It doesn't matter how sustainable an item is, first and foremost it must be desirable, wearable, and practical.

As a customer, the single biggest thing I consider when I buy an item is, will I get a good Cost Per Wear? Yes, we have come full circle!

It doesn't matter how eco the fabric is, or how little waste was derived from the manufacturing process, or how much the worker was paid. Yes, these factors matter to me and are part of my decision-making process. But I would never buy an item solely because of them. I refuse to be made to feel bad about buying something I really love, and I will wear for years to come, just because it's not from a specialist 'sustainable brand'. Many of my most loved and most worn clothes are from High Street chains.

I'm often asked, why sustainable or independent small brands are more expensive. The answer is in part related to general economies of scale, and in part related to the increased costs of labour and/or materials. By their nature, independent brands sell fewer products than chain stores, and so the quantities they buy from factories are comparatively low, leaving them with little buying power when negotiating. Small production runs equal high overheads. A lot of the cost of producing a garment, in fact in producing almost any product, is in the research, development, and sampling stages. If a brand produces 10,000 or 100,000 dresses, those initial set up and development costs are spread across the volume of the order.

Small brands incur many of the same set up costs but if they only manufacture a couple of hundred dresses, that is a lot of overhead per dress. Big brands benefit from economies of scale that come from large production runs which is reflected in the selling prices.

In order to differentiate, independent brands often use more premium materials or materials that carry a reduced environmental impact. These fabrics and trims, again bought in small quantities, come with a premium price tag. Many factories are not geared up for short production runs – they just can't do it profitably, and those that can are usually smaller, sometimes family owned. These factories, like the brands differentiate themselves by offering a point of difference. Often it can be good ethical and environmental standards and practices, for example, pay workers better wages or living wages, offer staff perks such as onsite childcare, a good canteen proving nutritious food. Perhaps they can offer accreditations such as Organic and Fair Trade. None of these come cheaply and so the price it costs to manufacture in a factory like that, is higher.

At the other end of the scale, I am also asked, how can a retailer only sell it for that much? My reply, as the saying goes, is "*if something seems to be too good to be true, it usually is.*" If 'fastfashion.com' is selling a dress for a fiver, even someone with little knowledge of the industry and only basic arithmetic, can work out that something doesn't add up.

The cost of clothing is not just how much a retailer pays a factory, there are a whole host of hidden or not so hidden costs to include,

CASH RECEIPT

Address: Any fashion store, your town centre, any country

- -

Date: 09-11-2021	10.35
Design costs	£
Sample costs	£
Fabric	£
Trim costs	£
Transport	£
Labour	£
Testing	£
QC	£
Logistics	£
Tax & Duties	£
Distribution costs	£
Retail costs	£
Profit	£
Total	**Selling price**

Buying sustainable fashion can be a rich (wo)man's game and many of my friends are confused and conflicted. Naturally they want to buy new clothes and of course they don't intentionally want to exploit workers or the environment, but the reality is they are busy women with a limited budget. They need affordability and convenience.

Throughout this book I have championed preloved as the most sustainable and scalable solution. It's something we can all do and our actions will have immediate impact. If one million women bought their next piece of clothing second hand instead of new, we would save 6 million kgs of carbon pollution from entering the atmosphere.[3] But shopping second-hand can be limiting, when your size is not available or what you want isn't for sale. So, in what other ways can you dress more sustainably without breaking the bank, and the planet?

There has been an explosion in the clothing rental market, in 2009 Jennifer Hyman and Jennifer Fliess co-founded, Rent the Runway, an e-commerce platform that allows users to rent, subscribe, or buy designer apparel and accessories. According to Hyman,

---

3 Home - Ethical Hour | Ethical Business Community

"*It was a paradigm-shift, away from the industry's old model of exclusion and waste, encouraging women to spend too much and toss too soon*". It was hugely successful, and in October 2021 was the first female founded, CEO, COO and CFO business to IPO.

Women are changing the way they consume clothes, no longer is it seen essential to own an item. There's a growing demand from consumers, especially in relation to occasion wear, which, as we discovered back in chapter one, tends to have a high cost per wear that the business model is being replicated all over the world.

Another more sustainable approach, that is growing in popularity amongst brands and consumers is the made to order model. This pre order concept forgoes the need for inventory, and by making only what is already sold, it reduces waste and eliminates deadstock.

A few years ago, I was working as a freelance stylist for a Hong Kong brand who introduced this model. Back then, it was commerciality rather than sustainability that was the driving force behind this. Carrying less inventory and still being able to offer the customer a wide range of options, in terms of print and silhouettes, made commercial sense. It would not have been viable for a small business to stock all the possible permutations.

The garments were not inexpensive, these were considered purchases that customers were happy to wait for, especially knowing the item was made just for them.

This concept is becoming increasingly popular, especially as technology advances. Scandinavian brands in particular are embracing this method. Even fashion ecommerce site ASOS have launched ranges using new technology, which enables them to print and manufacture on demand and in the UK. This avoids long lead times and high minimum order quantities. As innovation in this field advances, I believe this is a strategy that more brands will explore, especially with the re-shoring of some manufacturing. Fashion really is cyclical!

One of the challenges the fashion industry faces, is its lack of transparency within its supply chain. Having the confidence that garments are being made in approved factories, who meet each brands internal code of conduct, is the first step in avoiding malpractices such as, child labour, forced labour, and unsafe working conditions. But monitoring this effectively takes investment and commitment. Travel restrictions brought about by Covid-19 have made this challenge all the harder in recent times.

Many brands have good visibility of their primary suppliers, meaning the factories producing their finished garments, but the deeper into the supply chain you delve, the less clear it becomes. Brands can't monitor what they don't know and often, the how, where, and by who, the fabric, trims, and packaging are produced is not always clear. In addition, the practice of subcontracting (placing an order with a particular factory, who then offload it to another, usually cheaper factory, for production without prior agreement) is not uncommon. This is full of risk.

In a bid to solve this challenge, block chain technology is starting to be used as a tool for greater transparency and traceability. The luxury sector is embracing this technology, LVMH, Prada Group, and Richemont are founding members of Aura Blockchain Consortium, a Swiss based non-profit, which tracks and traces a products entire lifecycle, from raw material through to resale. This is vital in verifying the supply chain but is also particularly useful in authenticating these high value goods as well as preventing counterfeiting and aiding the ever growing resell market.

Innovation is happening and technologies are improving but to capitalise on these, we also need the human will to change, businesses need to move from a can do, to a must do, mindset. Of course, as consumers we can make changes, but alone, it won't be enough. We also need better regulation and government intervention.

Buying less and buying well should be encouraged, by reducing the amount we collectively buy we encourage the retailers to slow down and produce less. But what about when we do want to buy that something that is brand new.

As with most things in life, money talks.

Every time you spend money, you are ***casting a vote for the kind of world you want.***

ANNA LAPPE

You should never underestimate the amount of power you have as a consumer. Vote with your wallet. You have more influence than you realise. By not buying poorly made, short shelf-life clothes (or any items for that matter) then companies will cease to make them. Supply and demand - it's a principle as old as time.

If possible, shop locally, money made in the local economy tends to stay in the local economy, creating jobs and keeping the wealth within communities. When you can, consider supporting businesses who take responsibility and whose values align with your own, instead of buying from brands who treat their staff and supply chain poorly.

Ask questions of the brands or do your homework on them, you can check out the Fashion Transparency Index[4] where 250 of the world's largest fashion brands are reviewed and ranked according to the information they disclose about their social and environmental policies. By demanding transparency, organisation like Fashion Revolution believe it enables those advocating for change to identify abuses and work with brands to better track and manage governance risks that may affect not only

4 FASHION TRANSPARENCY INDEX 2021 - Fashion Revolution : Fashion Revolution

workers but the brands themselves. Without pressure from people like us, the retailers have no incentive to change.

When Fast Fashion brands bring out more sustainable ranges, (and of course, only if you like the clothes) buy them, it demonstrates that consumers care and there's a market for more sustainable options, the more brands sell the more they will invest in and develop these ranges. If we stop buying crap, retailers will stop making crap.

Dressing sustainably is becoming a middle-class privilege. What I see happening in sustainable fashion now, is reminiscent of the food industry, when buying organic became fashionable and a sign of status. Of course, organic food is better for our bodies and our planet, but sadly it is not affordable to all. When you have a family to feed on a limited budget, ethics are of little or no relevance, feeding your family takes priority. I worry that fashion is going the same way. I am witnessing an increased snobbery and a subtle (or not so subtle), sneering of people that wear some cheap or Fast Fashion brands. Buying second hand can be a lifestyle choice, many preloved boutiques focus on high end and designer brands, while they often offer great value, they are rarely 'cheap'. People who can afford not to have to, may love to rummage in a charity shop but those who rely on them do not always take the same pleasure. For many people, access to clothes that don't result in bullying or being stigmatised can be a godsend, especially for those on low incomes or with financial pressures.

This book is not about guilt or shaming or making us feel bad for our choices. Goodness knows how many times over the years that I have bought clothes online at a price that is too good to be true, shopped in shops whose ethics may not align with my own. Over the years, as I have learnt more, my values and priorities have changed. I hope that this book has helped you to understand that choices exist and the way you spend every dollar or pound matters. I adopt a 'every little helps' mantra for a reason. If one million of us spent fifty pounds with a company whose values aligned with our own, that equals £50m going to businesses who will invest in their staff, their supply chain and produce more responsibility. For me, that is a pretty good alternative.

Consume less;
share better.

HERVE KEMPF

Final Thoughts

The fashion industry is just one of many that finds itself at a junction. It can pivot towards a cleaner, fairer, and more sustainable model or it can continue as it is, focused on increasing consumption and maximising profit over people and the planet. I'm hopeful the majority within it will choose the former.

The discussion of sustainability within the fashion industry is now mainstream but when I started my career, I don't ever recall the word being used, and it definitely wasn't part of any departmental KPIs! Twenty years later, I very much doubt there is a major retailer who hasn't employed a whole department, whose job it is, to improve environmental and social practices, and effectively market them to stakeholders.

This is a good thing, the more retailers and manufacturers engaged and invested in improving, the quicker we'll see real change. Some solutions are expensive and naturally there is plenty of opposition, but we as shoppers must do our part. By voting with our money, we communicate our preferences. If we demand change, those businesses who want to thrive will have to meet our demands in the long term.

While clothing is regarded in our collective psyche as disposable, rather than something to be kept for life, we will struggle to make a real difference. Changing attitudes is as much of a challenge as changing labour practices, corporate behaviour, and international laws. Improving awareness and delivering better education around the subject is critical in empowering consumers to make more informed decisions. Organisations such as Redress, Fashion Revolution, and the Ellen MacArthur Foundation have been doing this for many years, and it is amazing to see their influence and reach grow.

While some of us may be willing, or able, to pay more for garments that are more sustainable, the ultimate goal should be for these to be accessible for all. With scale comes real impact. Small brands alone cannot move the needle. Investment in new technologies is key, in all areas of the product cycle from farming methods, to designing out waste, to logistics and finally how we as wearers consume, every stage leaves a footprint.

To facilitate better decision making and to become more sustainable, brands need to understand their environmental footprint and be able to identify areas of high impact. Ten years ago, the Sustainable Apparel Coalition was founded, a non-profit with a vision to create an industry that gives more than it takes – to the planet and its people. Made up of over 250 member organizations from 36 counties, comprising of retailers, suppliers, non-profits, and brands, it developed The Higg Index, an apparel and footwear industry self-assessment standard for assessing environmental and social sustainability throughout the supply chain. Covering topics such as water use, carbon emissions, and labour conditions.

As greenwashing persists and people become dubious of retailers' sustainability claims, many brands are seeing the business case for achieving meaningful accreditation, that demonstrates to consumers that their actions reflect their words. One such option is Benefit Corporation, known as B-Corp and often referred to as the 'gold standard' of sustainability. It is well known within the industry, but I genuinely question if the average shopper is even familiar with, never mind understands what achieving this status entails or means.

Awarded by B-Lab, achieving B-Corp status represents meeting a stringent level of social, environmental, and corporate governance. Certified businesses are legally required to consider the impact of their decisions on their workers, customers, suppliers, community, and the environment. Chloe has just become the first luxury brand to achieve B-Corp status and the talk from retailers, at every price point, is about how they can operate more responsibly. But the benefits that this kind of certification delivers must be understood by the general public in order to change consumer behaviour.

We need to encourage more collective discussion and understanding around how our clothes are really made and discarded. Only with improved education and realistic alternatives do I believe we will all choose consciously. The solutions are expensive and naturally there is plenty of opposition, but without doubt, moving society towards sustainable consumption is vital.

As we all know now, sustainability within fashion is complicated, there are no easy solutions and 'right' ways of shopping, but I hope reading this book has inspired you to think, and shop, differently. Curating a guilt-free wardrobe is possible, just follow these steps and you will be helping to create a fashion industry fit for the future.

1. Buy fewer brand-new clothes, make sure you really love them, and then wear them for longer.
2. When you are looking to add to your wardrobe, consider second had first.
3. Spend your money with retailers whose values align with your own, and whose actions speak lounder than their marketing campaigns.

I will leave you with a quote from sustainability advocate Brooke Bowlin, "*Intention is the root of sustainability for individuals… It gives us direction in our decision making. It gives us conviction in our actions, and it gives us purpose to pursue better, even if it requires deviating from our previous practices*"

Like in all aspects of life, to create meaningful change it takes many of us, all making small changes to our habits, we don't need to be perfect, we just need to start.

Let's be the change.

Wear clothes that tell ***a real story.***

About The Author

For over twenty years Sheryl has worked across many areas of the fashion industry. Having held Buying, Sourcing and Product Development roles in the UK and Asia for some of the world's leading retailers and small independent brands, she understands first-hand what goes into making the clothes we wear.

In 2013 Sheryl founded a Hong Kong based wardrobe editing service, and has worked with many women, some of whom were frustrated and disillusioned by clothes shopping and the fashion industry in general, to bring practical solutions to their sartorial problems.

Becoming a parent changed her perspective on the industry, she became increasingly concerned about the negative impact of fashion and her focus shifted towards working with those who want to create solutions. She has advocated for and worked with NGOs and charities that work to reduce fashions' negative impact. In 2020, Sheryl graduated from Hong Kong University with an

Executive Certificate in Corporate Social Responsibility.

For more than a decade she has organised numerous charity 'Frock Swaps' and more recently has written for various online publications and her own website www.makemywardrobework.com on the topics of sustainable consumption and wardrobe editing. Her everyday musings can be found on Instagram @ makemywardrobework

Acknowledgements

I've wanted to write this book for so long and making it happen has been a true passion project. So many people have given their time and talents unconditionally but without one person it would not have been possible, Lisa Beattie, thank you not only for believing in the project but for your hard work, encouragement and honesty while editing this book. From that first Frock Swap back in 2011 you have shared my love of preloved and I can't thank you enough for your support.

Irene Brown, thank you for your commitment to creating a cover to be proud of. Claire Yates thank you for your advice, support, and continuous encouragement to 'get it done'. To Kirsty Sullivan for reading and re reading, across the miles! To David, Annabelle and Lucas for the support and space to be able write this, I love you. To all my friends who committed to pre ordering copies, thank you for your generosity.

Rhea Lajom, it was a pleasure to work with you again and Elvina Choi, I'm so glad to enable your first published illustrations, thank you for your patience when I needed yet another revision!

To all the team at Jump, Samantha, Josie, and Emily, I know this project has been unique! I am so grateful for your honesty, creative genius and for always bearing with me when the process seemed overwhelming. I really hope you are as proud of the final outcome as I am.

Thank you, reader, for taking the time, it means so much.

RESOURCES

1 BBC Earth
2 BBC News
3 Boston Consulting Group (www.bcg.com)
4 Business Insider
5 Business News Daily
6 Business of Fashion
7 China Daily
8 Collins English Dictionary
9 Drapers Record
10 Forbes
11 Grazia International.
12 Hong Kong Home Affairs Department
13 Labour Behind the Label
14 Mintel
15 Oxford English Dictionary
16 Retail Week
17 Reuters
18 The Fair-Trade Foundation
19 The Guardian
20 The Liverpool Echo
21 The New York Times
22 The United Nations Development Programme (www.undp.org)
23 The University of Plymouth.ac.uk
24 The Wall Street Journal
25 United Nations IPCC Climate Report, 2021.
26 United States Environmental Protection Agency
27 Vogue
28 Women's Wear Daily
29 www.air-threads.com
30 www.ariel.co.uk
31 www.bangladeshaccord.org
32 www.bangladeshworkersafety.org
33 www.canopyplanet.org
34 www.cleanclothes.org
35 www.electrolux.hr
36 www.ellenmacarthurfoundation.org
37 www.ethicaltrade.org
38 www.fashionista.com
39 www.fashionnetwork.com
40 www.fashionrevolution.org
41 www.fashionrevolution.org
42 www.futurefashionfactory.org
43 www.kering.com
44 www.mckinsey.com
45 www.parliament.co.uk
46 www.oerlikon.com
47 www.oxfam.org.au
48 www.oxfam.org.uk
49 www.primark.com
50 www.redress.com.hk
51 www.thefashionpact.org
52 www.thredup.com
53 www.vice.com
54 www.weforum.org
55 www.wrap.org.uk
56 www.yougov.co.uk